permanence

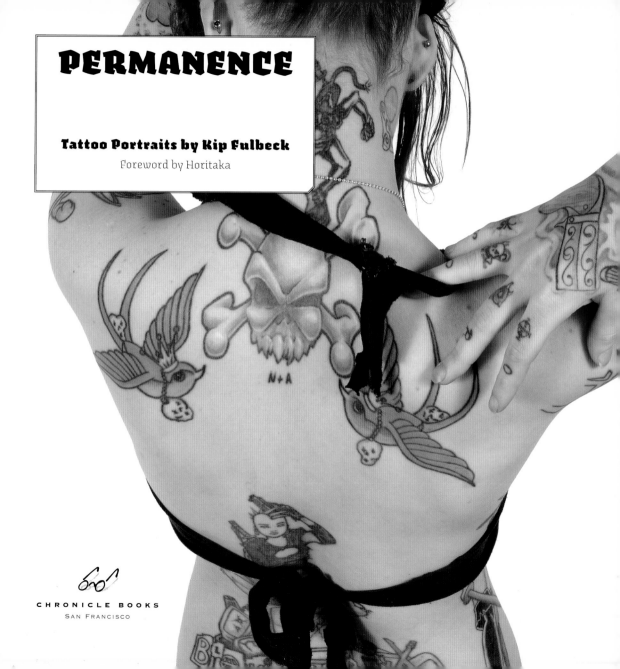

PERMANENCE

Tattoo Portraits by Kip Fulbeck

Foreword by Horitaka

CHRONICLE BOOKS
SAN FRANCISCO

Library of Congress Cataloging-in-Publication
Data available.

ISBN: 978-0-8118-6131-1

Manufactured in China.
Designed by Brett MacFadden.

10 9 8 7 6 5 4 3 2 1

Chronicle Books LLC
680 Second Street
San Francisco, CA 94107

www.chroniclebooks.com

Acknowledgments

My thanks and love to my parents and family for their constant support, even when I fled premed for a lifetime of making art, buying guitars, getting tattooed, and pursuing other things not listed on the Asian family "to do" list.

Thanks to the many friends who helped out with this project: Kris Andrews, Lindsay Castro, Jonathan Cecil, Tim Connelly, Adam Day, Seymour Duncan, Al and France Garcia, Manny Garcia, Jim Goldberg, Mariko Gordon, Jake Jacobson, Ethan Kaplan, Carianne Laguna, Rachel Lithgow, Horacio Martinez, Quinn Messmer, Saudia Mills, Dan "The Nazz" Nazzareta, Paul Nelson, Permanent Mark, Ken Phillips, Kara Richardson, Jessica Sonquist, Joey Souza, Splinter and Diablo, Tim Stephens, Kellie Stoelting, Tian Tang, Josh Thomas, Tynisa Winslow, the staffs of the Japanese American National Museum and the UCSB Department of Art, and the UCSB Academic Senate for its generous support.

Thank you again to the wonderful crew at Chronicle Books—particularly Brett MacFadden, Patti Quill, and my amazing (and patient) editor, Bridget Watson Payne. Thanks to my superagent, Faye Bender; my multivernaculared research assistant, Jessica Hulce; and my students, who are a never-ending source of challenge and reality checks. Thank you to Phel Steinmetz for being my teacher always. And thank you to Horitomo, Horitaka, and Horiyoshi III Sensei, for honoring me with their work; with particular thanks to Horitaka for his friendship and guidance.

My special thanks to Michael Velasquez for his generosity, vision, and skill; and to my lovely wife, Heather, for her strength, loyalty, and caring.

I am indebted to each and every individual who took the time to share their bodies and stories for this project, opened their homes and businesses to me, offered words of encouragement and support, and found meaning in personal narrative. *Vita non est vivere sed valere vita est.*

Foreword

Why do you do it? This may in fact be one of the most common questions directed at the tattooed, and is closely related and just as confusing as the question "What does it mean?" And there is no easy or all-conclusive answer. People get tattooed for a wide spectrum of reasons—group identity, lack of group identity, joy, sorrow, hate, love, drunken stupor, insecurity, security, affirmation. . . . The reasons are endless, and as varied as human nature, imagination, and emotion.

I began collecting tattoos when I was in high school, and at that time I think they were connected to a variety of motivating factors. Though I find it hard to pinpoint exactly (teenage rebellion and art appreciation were certainly influential reasons), I do know that I just wanted them. And since then, I have continued to collect . . . sometimes in commemoration of an event or time, to mark friendship or love, or maybe to prove something to myself. Oftentimes, I have been tattooed in order to receive a tattoo from a particular person. This exchange often has nothing to do with art, but more with friendship or respect. There have been a few of these done by people who are not tattooers and ended up doing their first, and probably only, tattoo on me. Other

times, I have simply admired tattoo art. And despite what the TV programs tell you, no one has to die for you to get tattooed. Tattoos can have some deep profound meaning, but they don't have to. I would remind people to take what they see on TV or read in books with a grain of salt.

So why do we do it? It seems like this is a topic that is overdiscussed and overanalyzed, particularly in the "scholarly" arena. Being a tattooed person and a tattooer focusing on the Japanese style of art myself, I came across one such conjecture that strikes me as grossly unfair and worthy of rebuttal.

Early Chinese reports and archaeological findings evidence Japanese tattoos and body arts dating back thousands of years. In the current world of Japanese tattooing, the bodysuit design affecting the appearance of a large area of the body is salient. The roots of this current incarnation of Japanese tattooing are in popular arts of the Edo period (1603–1867). There is speculation and debate about the origins of this type of tattooing, and I repeatedly hear scholarly theories asserting that the large style of tattooing was created in order to cover and hide penal tattooing. It is true that the Japanese government once employed what is probably one of history's grossest misuses of the tattoo needle—tattooing those convicted with marks designating their alleged crimes. And because of this legacy, one can easily see how such a theory developed.

I find this theory to be particularly insulting, pessimistic, and laden with scholarly arrogance . . . arrogance combined not only with a large amount of ignorance of the tattoo profession, but also with no attempt at gaining understanding from an insider perspective. This happens largely because, until very recently, writings about tattooing rarely came from within the community and did not include the knowledge of a member of a group (in this case an underground group— by the way, that's *underground,* not *underworld*). While I freely agree that individuals who were tattooed to cover "convict marks" existed—as they do now—I find the notion that a beautiful art form was simply created as a disguise, or the implication that all of the tattooed were criminals, to be quite derisive. Ironically, if one studies diagrams of said penal tattooing marks, many are on the forehead and simply could not be covered with larger tattoo work. The majority of other marks are solid black armbands of varying number and size, slightly similar to the "black tribal armband" tattoo popular in the '90s in America. And as any working tattooer will tell you, these are quite difficult to cover well. Even in this era, with improved inks and the use of machines, masking solid black bands is a tall order. The covering of penal tattoos in old Japan probably existed, however poorly, but noncriminal firemen, artisans, and laborers were among those who celebrated tattooing as well.

Scholars tend to want to quantitatively analyze and understand everything, and there is a value to this. However, how do you quantitatively analyze a love song? Or why a certain painting may move you to tears? At their best, tattoos can be seen and appreciated as an art form. I think in some cases, such as in the Japanese tattoo, tattooing can even transcend art and embody a culture. But I don't think this is a requirement. Certainly not all tattoos can qualify in that manner—nor do they have to. They can just be enjoyed. Tattoos, for better or worse, reflect the human experience. Our successes, joys, mistakes, and failures are all recorded on our skins. And just like life itself, sometimes they aren't perfect. Sometimes they're even tragic. But they are real. A tattoo is just ink in skin . . . it is up to the bearer to ascribe a meaning or value to it.

And while Kip Fulbeck, decorated, published, and tenured as he may be, is in fact a scholar himself, his approach with this book was one of a field researcher—or, more important, of a human.

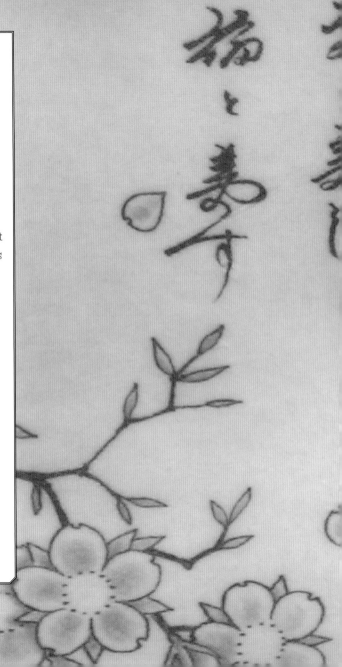

He documents and presents without judgment, a necessary factor when hoping to elicit an honest response. He also approaches the project as an insider himself, one of the ranks of the tattooed, and is less restricted by outside prejudices. And I think you will find his research to cover a wide spectrum, the answers being as simple or as complicated as the human psyche itself. What follows is truly an honest response to the question of *why*.

With regard to tattoos . . . me personally? I just think they're cool and I still love them as much as I did in high school.

Horitaka (Takahiro Kitamura)
San Jose, California

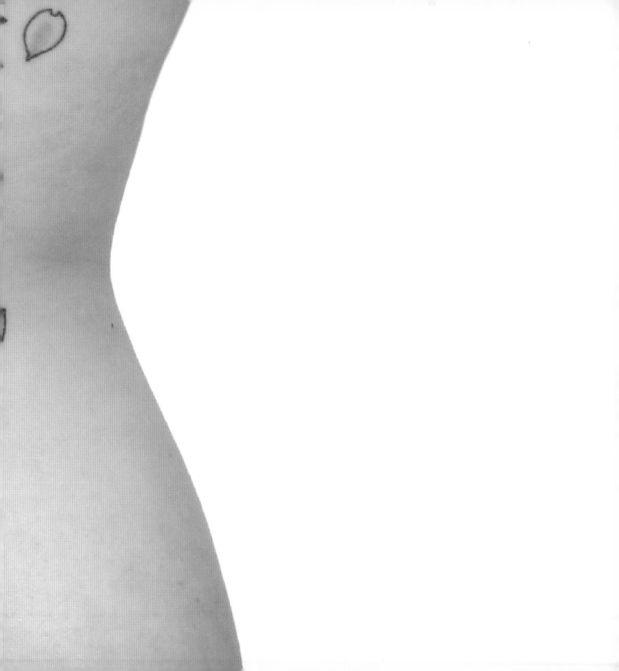

Introduction

When I teach my college art seminars, I start the first class by asking each student to tell the group something unique about themselves—or, as I put it, something *nontransferable*. What I'm looking for is a random fact, a salient feature, an off-the-wall quirk that separates them from the Xeroxed pack of names, majors, and ID numbers blurring my roll sheet each year. I'm looking for something that makes them *them*. Part of this is an exercise in thinking for themselves and part of it is a gimmick for me to help keep their names fresh for the next ten weeks until I can Ctrl+Alt+Delete them and start over. Since we already spend our lives individualizing ourselves, the task should be simple. We all customize our behavior and appearance every day—our dress, our gait, our vernaculars, our possessions, even our tastes. The exercise starts and we go around the room, giving each person a turn. "I don't know any of you," I say, "so give me something that makes you stand out. Tell me something that's yours."

"I love playing soccer" doesn't work. Boring. Neither does "I come from a family of six" or "I'm obsessed with Ashlee Simpson." Invariably, someone else has the same family size or the same questionable taste. Try again.

I tell them each of us has our own histories; our immensely varied and private experiences to cull from that are completely and absolutely our own. And because of this—because we have all lived different lives, eaten different foods, kept different dogs or cats or fish or birds or monkeys, kissed different people, made different mistakes, bought different shoes, watched different movies, told different lies—finding something unique about ourselves, something utterly our own, should be easy. Sure, sometimes we get caught in a fad, finding a commonality of iPod ownership or *Project Runway* watching, but the vast majority of our lives are completely and idiosyncratically ours and ours alone. So tell me something nontransferable.

At this point, I'm usually met with uncomfortable and prolonged silence—every teacher's nightmare, complete with poker faces, spiral notebooks, and fresh pens. Until eventually, a brave alpha or two will venture forward into the conceptual abyss, tentatively volunteering a particular fondness for fondue parties, or detailing the gory particulars of a recent relationship breakup or a youth spent with a bipolar mother. Something we actually find memorable, even intriguing. Something we actually want to know more about. When this happens, and it happens every class sooner or later, the group as a whole takes its first step in differentiating what really interests us from what we're supposed to care about when we ask someone how they're doing. And occasionally in this exercise, rather than say anything at all, a student will simply stand up, lift their shirt or roll up their pant leg, and show us their tattoo. Then things really start to cook. It doesn't matter if we like the ink or not. Everyone wants to know *why*.

There are forty million people with ink in the United States alone, and thousands more every day. Forty million different reasons for choosing to permanently mark our bodies. Forty million different answers to the question. You can go to most any town in America now and get inked. Pick up a magazine, turn on the television, or go to the gym and the person next to you has a tattoo. What was once a bastion of nonconformity is now mainstream, the same way Reagan era–led youth incarceration eventually brought baggy denims to the Gap and the word *punk* moved from describing the working-class anger of early Clash and Sex Pistols to the barre chords and pop harmonies of the latest Green Day clone.

It's like I dozed off for a second and missed the middle chapters. All of a sudden we're in Act III and someone is talking about the ides of March. A random Justin Timberlake is onstage singing black-inspired music, dressed in clothes inspired by black prison youth, wearing ink inspired by generations of sailors, bikers, criminals, and other social outcasts with a million hot girls cheering him on, and no one seems to care. No one bats an eye. No one even asks if it bothers me.

These are easy things to complain about, but complaining about them just gets you pegged as old and cantankerous and I'm already in my forties. I might as well be yelling at kids to get off the front lawn, complaining about those damn skateboarders, and misplacing my coupons while standing in line at Rite Aid. It's easier just to roll with it. Tattoos are everywhere, and counting.

Maybe it's a perceived lack of individuality in a world of Starbucks, Circuit City, Carl's Jr., and Olive Garden. Maybe it's the absence of meaningful rituals within our modern culture (quick: name me something meaningful about your high school graduation). Maybe it's as simple as a love of a historically dismissed art form finally being recognized and accepted by the masses. Or maybe it's really, as I'm often told, just another trend like straight-leg jeans, silver cars, Bluetooths you have to scream in to be heard, and those horrible Croc shoes. Except this one you can't pitch on eBay after your visiting cousin copies you.

Trends come and go like sudoku books, and while tattooing one's body can now be as easy as an impulsive trip to the local strip mall, both the reality and the art form's history involve much more than that. Anyone, if they want it bad enough, can come up with the money and bear the physical pain of getting inked. But money and pain aren't the issues. Whether we realize it or not at the time, choosing to get tattooed transforms you—sometimes innocuously, other times with profound significance. The process itself can be purging—a way to memorialize a life event or person, or an attempt to navigate an emotional experience. It can be a bonding between friends, a display of aggression or of belonging or not belonging, a revered adornment, an abhorrent branding, or simply the visual evidence of nothing more than a whim caught at the right place at the right time. Whatever the circumstance, one constant remains present. Getting tattooed transforms how others view you, and often how you see yourself as well. As a friend once told me after my first ink, "You're no longer Kip now. You're Kip with tattoos."

I don't feel any particular kinship with other tattooed people, any more than I have some inherent commonality with someone just because they're American or they enjoy surfing. Some people I like. Some I admire. Some I'm embarrassed of. Most I ignore. I'll be the first to admit I don't care about most tattoos I see. A lot of hasty decisions being made, and a plethora of questionably skilled practitioners putting out loads of shoddy work (the better to offset the several dozen amazingly talented tattooers out there, I suppose). But what I do like, what I have always liked, are the stories behind our decisions. What makes us how we are—how we dress, how we talk, who we're attracted to (and who we're repelled by . . . the whole would-you-rather-do _____ or _____ game). And particularly, what drives someone to permanently mark their body. The individual reasoning, the thought process behind why we choose to be tattooed—where on our body we do it, what style and design we settle on, and who we trust with the process.

I want to know why someone walks by a tattoo shop and spontaneously decides to enter, pick some flash off the wall, pay whoever happens to be working, and walk out an hour later bandaged while others read books, attend conventions, and interview tattooers for decades before ever getting their first tattoo (if they ever do get one). Why do some people tattoo their lover's name on their chest and others their favorite automobile manufacturer? Why do some feel the urge to immerse themselves in a foreign culture's historical tradition while others choose to create their own or simply FTW? Then again, I wonder why people read *The Da Vinci Code* instead of Salinger, why they wear cowboy hats in cities and care what Tom Cruise's baby looks like, why more people know Flavor Flav from some insipid reality show than remember the sheer brilliance of Public Enemy (actual student comment: "He used to be in a band?"). Maybe I just have one of those brains you can't turn off.

I photographed hundreds of people for this book from all walks of life, from Chelsea to Compton, asking them to tell me about their tattoos. Asking them to tell me their stories. Asking that question *why*. Maybe you'll find some of the images or the stories interesting, or meaningful. Maybe you'll see something about yourself in another's image or writing. Maybe you'll admire someone's artwork, ridicule someone's mistake, or be inspired by another's courage. I'd like to think some of these will make an impact on you, but if not, that's okay. It's not my deal, not my story. It's nontransferable. It's theirs.

Kip Fulbeck
Santa Barbara, California

After a close encounter with a 8ft Bull Shark we made a deal. Sharks don't eat me & I won't eat them.

I got my first tattoo when I was
16 — stupid kid! The praying mantis
set has a feminist undercurrent but
I am NOT a bra-burner. Really.
The Buddha in the center of my chest
is a shout-out to my Chinese family
overseas who I have never met and
probably will.

The maneki neko? My grandmother
had them displayed left & right in
her Chinatown apartment when I'd
visit her every Saturday as a kid.
Her funeral was the only one I
have ever cried at.

koei-kan
Place of Peace & Prosperity

I got it when they were stripping me of my Black belt for starting to compete in kickboxing. it was a "Fuck you" to them. They cant take something I earned!

Your heart may crack a little, but don't let it break in half. Let your family be your true love. My beautiful family tartan was done by Jeff Rassier of Blackheart Tattoo.

Kiss 76/77 changed my life.
Seeing them live put me on a
path that I have never
strayed from.
The Demon possessed me and
has not let go.
Thanks Gene ♪

I am CALM, my sister Britnea is a BEAM, and my baby sister ~~Ashlea~~ Ashlea is A GEM. These are our initials, and we all act accordingly. I am an Aries and proud of it, but

I confused my tattoo artist when I asked for the Aryan symbol.

It's a truism that only _real_ marine biologists have tattoos. In fact, that's how you can tell the real ones from the wannabees.

The lower tat is a deepwater anglerfish. The large fish is the female, the little stubby thing is the male — it is a sexual parasite — every guy's dream.

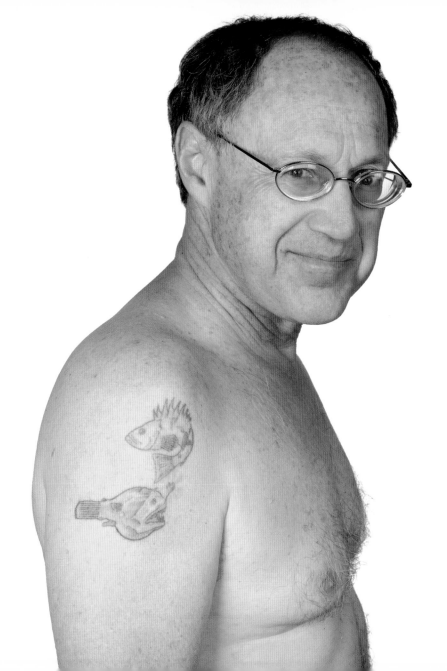

HELLO IM BettyNice ASPIRING PINUP
MODEL WITH NEN NEBSITE LAUNCHING
SOON. TATTOOS ARE MY LIFE AND
THE BEAUTIFUL WOMEN OF THE FIFTIE
ARE MY INSPIRATION WOMEN ARE
HOT ESPECIALLY WITH BEAUTIFUL
ART I LOVEY PINUP WITH A MODERN
TWIST.

MY T4T IS DEDECATEED to the women who
brot me in to this world.

WINNIE ADEL TYRELL
7-6-56 to 8·8·23

TATTOOING IS SUCH A GIANT PART of
MY LIFE, tHAt it's SO HARD TO tHINK
of tHE PERSON THAT I WOULD'NT BE
IF It HAD NOT BEEN SUch A StRONG
FActoR oveR tHE LASt 20 YEARS.
MY tAttoo's ARE ME & I Am MY
TAttOO'S EACH & EVER ONE of tHEM.
THANKS to EVERYONE who took tHĒ
Time withME.

PIX

PLAYING WITH BROKEN GUITARS.

UP ON HAIGHT STREET
IN THE CITY WITH SOME
FRIENDS. WALKED INTO A
TATTOO SHOP ON A WHIM.
STARTED TALKING WITH
JENNIFER, THE ARTIST.
ENDED UP SKETCHING
THE PIECE OUT MYSELF
& SHE DID IT
ON THE SPOT, LIKE BOOM,
                    F'REAL.

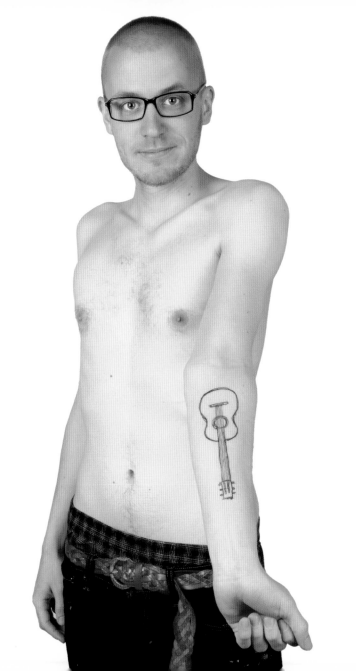

Being Raised in Indiana in a Baptist church tattoos ~~were~~ weren't smiled upon in my family.

I'm a writer who ~~suffers~~ suffers from extreme anxiety. I try to balance ~~of~~ out my creative energy. When I'm in a funk or stressed I write about Happy Stuff. And when I'm Happy I write about sad stuff. <u>Balance</u>. The four Hands on my heart are the strings that pull my anxiety cords

- Love
- Greed
- acquaintance's
- Enemies

korean pride, yo!
film for life!

oh snap.

I can't explain how much books mean
to me in this small space.
The pages are flying away to remind me
to let go.
The words on the pages are from one of my
favorite books, by Peter Beagle, but they've
blurred over the 15 years since I got this.
My belly tattoo was one of the things my
husband liked about me right away
when we met. Who gets a __book__ tattoo?
He values learning above almost anything
and that's what books represent to him.

The snake represents many things to many cultures. For me it's strength & protection over my heart.

Peace

"Shoulds"

My 1st TATTOO I GOT WHEN I WAS 17. IT's A CARTOON I MADE UP IN HIGH SCHOOL. HER NAME IS Shirley. — Its A LONG STORY.

[signature]

I always wanted a tattoo for as long as I can remember. When I finally decided to get one, I wanted it to have meaning. I started with a back piece of cherry blossoms to celebrate & signify my Japanese heritage. This was a huge decision because I knew my mother, being Japanese, would be completely against it. Four years later I added my Mon, or family crest to my chest.

I am proud of my lineage. I am proud of my tattoos. They represent my past present & future.

HELLS ANGELS FOREVER

I'm a little tired of the wearing turtleneck sweaters to family reunions in July — maybe I should send Mom + Dad this book for Christmas! Tattooing has provided me with the best things in life and I'd never change a thing! Let's hope I'm still invited to Christmas dinner next year!

xoxo
Nikki

Because sometimes things happen
that can't even be explained

I LOVE MY WIFE'S KISSES
CANT HAVE ENOUGH OF HER ♡.

THESE ARE my real lips like they
say "Till Death Do Us Apart"

Interview with Evan Seinfeld

Kip Fulbeck: Okay, you want to tell me about your tattoo history?
Evan Seinfeld: Oh shit.

Anything you want.
I grew up in Brooklyn, New York, where tattooing was illegal until the late '90s. The only guys who had tattoos were guys who had been in jail and older Italian guys—wiseguys. And most people got their tattoos from Tony Polito on Westridge Boulevard. I thought he only had four tattoos. He had the panther, the Christ head, the parrot, and the redheaded girl with her foot on the pirate chest. Being that I didn't really like any of those things I was never really going to get a tattoo.

I grew up in Canarsie and I was very into heavy metal and hardcore and punk. When I got into the hardcore scene in my teens, I started hanging out at CBGB's and going to L'amours and I started seeing amazing black work on people and I was immediately sucked in. And Billy, from my band, from Biohazard, he introduced me to Mike Perfetto—Michael Angelo—who did half my tattoos before I was even twenty.

Wow.
And it was, I remember it being kinda freakish to people because nobody had black-and-white tattoos. Nobody really had sleeves where I lived in New York. The only guys who really had sleeves were the Hells Angels and bikers, pretty much. And I've always ridden bikes, you know, but . . . it seems like it's become so mainstream now.

Yeah, tell me about that.
It's like, it seems like everybody is sure that they're not going to have to look for a bank job.

'Cause you're going on, like, year fifteen, right? Or more?
I'm thirty-eight. I started getting tattooed when I was eighteen. So twenty years, twenty-one years.

And how has that changed in terms of the reception?
Well, I just think now it's funny. Because you're in an elevator and *grandma's* gonna go, [in nasally voice] "Oh, look at you all tattooed! You look like 50 Cent, or Dennis Rodman."

You know, and that's the other thing, it's like black people never had tattoos until Dennis Rodman—like, almost like he started it. And, I don't know . . . I feel like people get tattoos for different reasons. People used to get tattoos to stand out. Now people get tattoos to fit in.

That's true.

It's funny. It's like if I were eighteen all over again and looking at what it looked like now, I probably wouldn't get tattooed the way I did because it would look more different to *not* get tattooed, in a weird way. You know, I'd probably choose something that was more like what you did—like a full back piece that nobody saw unless I wanted to show it to them.

So you wouldn't do your arms and stuff that shows?

No, because, it just seems that more times than not I wear long sleeves nowadays. You know, and even then, my neck and my head and my hands are tattooed so I can't ever really hide it. Not that I ever want to hide it—it's just that sometimes I don't feel like talking to people. And it seems like people feel a nervous obligation to strike up a conversation. And it's always in an elevator! It's always in an elevator. People feel really uncomfortable when they're alone with a tattooed person in an elevator. And they go, you know, what the fuck is people sayin' like, "Whoa, that's a lot of tattoos." I'm like, what kind of fuckin' idiotic statement is that? It's like, "Wow, you're really fat" or like, "Wow, you're really ugly" or, "Wow, look how shallow you are." You know, I really kinda refuse to get into those conversations.

Now, do they recognize you in the elevator?

You know, that's the other thing. People think you're a celebrity because you're on reality TV, then I'm like—"This is stupid." You know, it's like—

And they don't know you from music?

You know, it's funny. Biohazard was the biggest thing I ever did in my life, creatively. I did ten albums over nineteen years. And we sold four million records and we played in ninety countries around the world. Shit, we used to play three hundred shows a year. We may have played more concerts than anybody ever in kind of a weird way. And, you know, we used to *impact* people's lives because our lyrics were deep and spiritual and we talked about the strains of society at every level. Politically, socially, mentally, spiritually, physically. And we kinda created this kind of music driven—Biohazard was the urban soundtrack to, to, like, a modern-day young tribal ceremony. And we used to *bond,* and people would be in there, you know, slamming and letting out negative energy in a positive way. And more people know me that I slapped Sebastian Bach in a fuckin' stupid TV series. And like, they're *enamored* by that. And I'm just like, "Go buy a fuckin' record and read the lyrics. Oh, I'm sorry. Download it for free."

So when people meet you in elevators, is it usually because of the tattoos or because they recognize you?

No, the kind of people who strike up a conversation are people that are just like, they're scared that because you're tattooed that you're going to dismember them or something. I don't know where people get this kind of image in their mind, but it's pretty funny. You know, the only people I'll talk to are little old ladies. It's funny—they say "from the mouths of babes." I feel like kids and old people are really honest and everybody in the middle is usually full of shit.

So like, when you're in the supermarket— when me and Tera are in the supermarket, standing in line at fuckin' Whole Foods, waiting to get some fuckin' whatever we're getting . . . a four- or five-year-old kid will come over and touch my skin.

Yeah, I've had that happen.

Because, wow, look how interesting that is. And it's their parents who—

I like that, though.

Me, too! I think that's honest. They're inquisitive and they're trying to learn about life and they're interested in something different. And their parents who are in their forties are yanking that kid back and apologizing to you.

And I always say, "No, no. It's okay, come here, little boy." You know, why they're scared is none of my . . . I couldn't tell you. But little old ladies are the same thing. Little old ladies stop me in the supermarket, too. And they go, "What in the hell were you thinking? What does your mother think of that? Why would you do that? You're such a nice-looking boy. Why would you do that to your body?" You know?

So what do you say?

I don't have a stock answer for a question like that. I mean, you know, if a lil' old lady who seemed really sincere asked me that today, I would say, "You know, it was my body. It was my choice. It wasn't about my mom and it wasn't about God and it was just about me. It's my real estate and I'll decorate it how I want to." I'll appreciate their interest because it's genuine as opposed to someone who's just like, "Wow, you sure have a lot of tattoos." It's like, *what?* What is that?

It's like a nothing statement.

That's like saying, "Wow, you really are black."

[laughs] Yeah, I get that after I swim, in the showers. People are like, "Oh, wow, that's a lot of stuff."

You're like, "Really? I hadn't noticed."

I don't know what to say.

You know what? If I'm feeling really sarcastic, I do this bit where if someone goes, "Wow, that's a lot of tattoos." And I go, "What are you talking about?" And they go, "Your tattoos." And I go, "Oh my god! How did that get there?" You know? Stupid.

Could you talk really quick about your parents or about what they thought or about—

My parents . . . my parents are Jewish schoolteachers who were really put off by me getting tattooed. But they're pretty liberal and open-minded and I think once they got over the initial shock of the stigma they attached to it in *their* generation, 'cause they were coming off, you know, Holocaust survivors were the only Jews who had tattoos . . . My parents were born here in America. I'm born here in America. My kid's born here in America, you know? I wouldn't be surprised if my kid went and got tattooed. I hope he would consult me first—I'd make sure he gets the right artist.

Good point.

You know, I hope he doesn't come home with like, a Yu-Gi-Oh or a Pokémon tattoo!

Tattoo Culture has become so mainstream that I have mixed feelings about it. It seems like tattoos are now mandatory in Pop Culture for all musicians, athletes etc. I Remember when I was totally sleeved before it was fashionable. People were UNUSUALLY UNCOMFORTABLE. NOWADAYS PEOPLE FEEL OBLIGATED TO STRIKE UP A CONVERSATION IN ELEVATORS I JUST GIVE EM "THE LOOK" The difference between tattooed people and non tattooed people is that tattooed people DON'T CARE IF YOU DON'T HAVE TATTOO'S

F.W.

My tatoo is my dad's number from when he was in the concentration camp here in America. Everyone thinks it's a prison tattoo, but it was never meant that way... At first I was offended, but now I realize that in a way it is... Most of my friends like my tattoo, but the older people in the Japanese American community don't really like it or don't understand it. It makes me sad, because I'm doing it to honor them...not to exploit them... Maybe they'll get it eventually.

CANADIANS ROCK! JAY'S FINELINE TATTOOS KICKS FUCKIN' ASS!

S.F. SAN BRUNO
RULES!!! ~~FRANK!~~

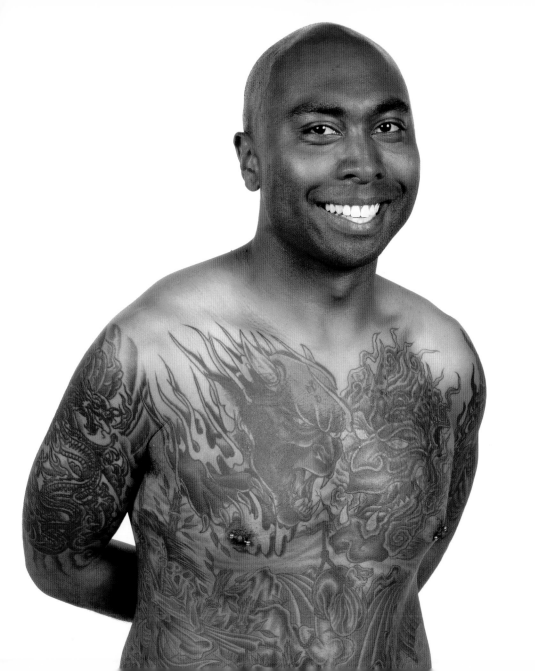

My grandmother owned a beauty salon in San Diego called Gina's Beauty Boutique. I was pretty young when she passed away, but I have great memories being at the shop with family, and having my Nana cut my hair.

She had an amazing light-box sign out front of the shop. I drew this tattoo from the shapes on the sign.

I guess remembering becomes a difficult thing to do. This tattoo helps me recall those memories, preserving their significance and making them a part of my life now - just more intensely.

Plus, the black ink really pops on the albinism skin!

At the age of 53 I was dared to get a tattoo so I did, it was great so it was the start of a full body suit now I finished at the age of 60 yrs It been fun, met my husband at a show. My tats are Indian theme.

Tat Chic

Joined the navy in 1967 got 2 tattoo the same night. I'm the perfect example of "tattoos are addictive. from my fingers to my little toe" :-)

Tat Man

This tattoo is in my memory of my cousin Robert, who died of Cancer in 2000 when he was 22. He was an awesome person and individual and will be missed by all. This tattoo is just a tribute to a great person who the the fullest of lives

Ride on

♡78 Forever

Women of Valor
Eva Brown
Daughter, Sister, Wife
Mother Grandmother
and Friend.

1927 –

Holocaust Survivor

A-17923

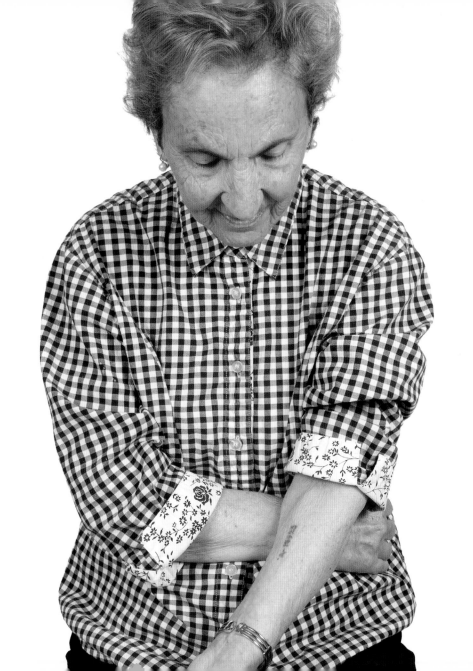

THIS IS A PORTRAIT OF MY MOM AROUND AGE 20 OF HER NURSING SCHOOL GRADUATION.

THIS IS ME AT AGE 37.

MY MOM TAUGHT ME HOW TO LOVE + CARE FOR PEOPLE & TO ALWAYS HAVE A TWINKLE IN MY EYE.
HER NAME WAS LAVEENA ANNE.

Harrison Detroit... The love of My life !!
That's what my neck says. I've had many
Ideas for my neck since my first tattoo fifteen
years ago — But Nothing Seemed Right. I Always
Considered this to be my most important tattoo —
the most meaningfull work on my body as it
would Represent my "Voice" as An Artist, as
a Mortal ... So I waited for the work to Reveal
itself to me, When Harrison was born on
Dec. 23rd that year, I knew by Christmas what
to Do. Harrison has come into my life & with
him brought an unimaginable world of love & peace
& infinite wisdom.
Through his being & my experience I have
Changed. Through that Change my "Voice" has
Changed.

I am a total rocker at heart, but I'm trying to keep my skin clean till after ~~I'm~~ my modeling career is over.

This is my only tatoo + I got the design from a shirt that I have. It took 2½ hours to complete + I wanted to die! My best friend told me that hers only stung a little.... Maybe I'm just a pussy, but mine hurt like hell! I tried talking to the artist, I tried watching tv + reading, nothing worked!

If you look closely, you can see that the butterfly is only shaded in. He did that to spare me another 45 minutes + for that, I thank him ☺

The pain quenched my ❌ tatoo thirst!

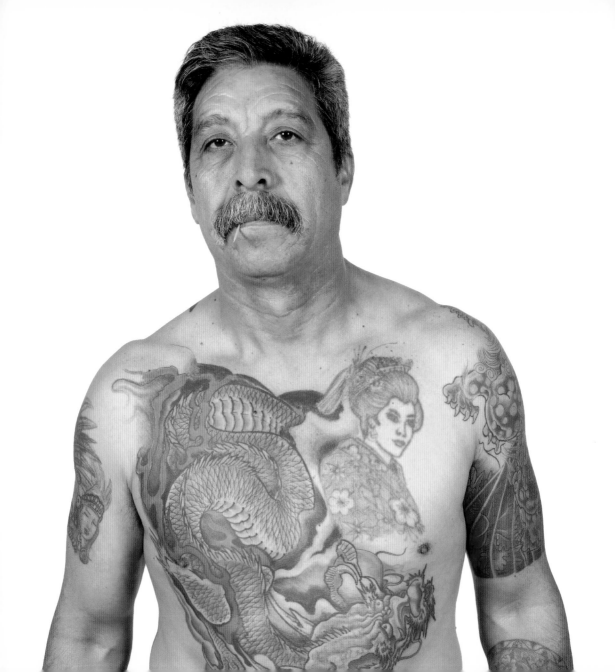

UNA ILUSION DE TODA LA
VIDA INICIADA EN 1967 MI
PRIMER TATUAJE Y despues de
35 AÑOS EMPIEZO OTRA VEZ
A TATUARME PIEZAS GRANDES
HECHAS POR EL ARTISTA EN
EL Estudio FU DOG ~~TATTOO~~ TATTOO
JESUS LEON ALIAS(CHUY)

I got Pasha cause
that's what my mom called me
all my life, so this tattoo
is for my mom (even though
she doesn't know I have it)
LOL !!!

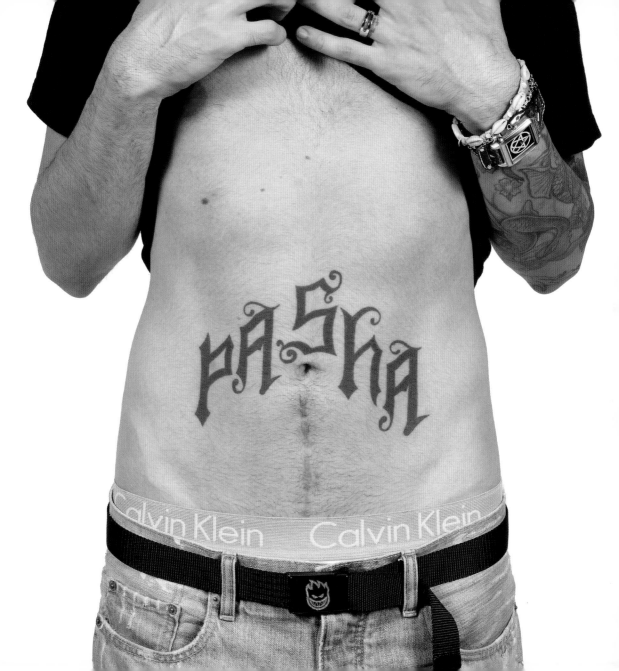

The headline on my
my myspace reads:
    "I've had sex before,
fake mustaches are way
better."

*on a side note: when I wear my mustache,
  I call myself Hector

When I was fifteen I got a tribal
armband. I ~~found~~ had no idea what
kind of ~~tattoo~~ I wanted, I just knew
I wanted one. It was 1993 and
I was in NYC (where I was born
+ raised, + still live) and tattooing
was illegal. So I went to an apt.
where a "tattooer" worked and was
talked into a tribal band. I happened
to have a school note book w/ my doodles
in it so we took one and made it into
the band. Being that I'm almost 30
I decided a few years ago that this
tribal band was no longer something I
enjoyed on my body so I covered it.

This is "Fish Ball Soup"

Yeup, it really says that; yeup it was on purpose.

This is my tribute to all those folks who found out too late that "Love & Happiness" actually said "Beef & Broccoli"

MR:BUGSY CPTS WSTOS
GOT THE AUBCTI/ ON ME
WHEN I WAS IN PRISON
WITH A HOME^(JAIL) MADE MACHINE
OUT OF A BROKEN WALMAN
AND A COUPLE OF OTHER SHT
JUST PASSING TIME.....chilling
WITH THE HOMIES. _

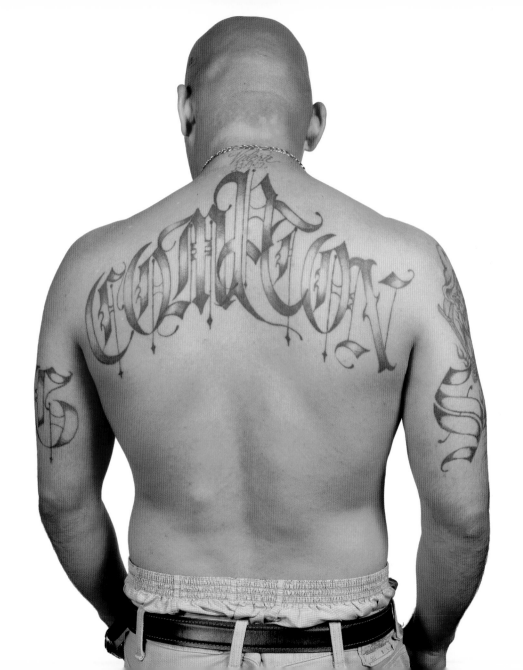

As a child my father and I attended many STREET Rodding Events. We would set up Booth next to Ed "Big Daddy" Roth. Now years AFTER BIG DADDY'S DEATH my Father and I have a pretty vast collection of Rat Fink memorabialia. Thanks Ed For being so kind To many children and Bringing many Fathers and sons Together!!

Travis Deckott

I got the tatoo
So that i could always Remember
my brother. He was killed by some
guy's awhile back. But the guy's that
did it, my brother new them but once he
was hit the guys that was with him just
left him lying there, No-one called for help
at all they just left. but they say he was lying
there at lease for like 30 minutes. but if some
one would have called for help when it happenel
my brother would still be alive today.

Interview with Kat Von D

Kip Fulbeck: Tell me how you first got into tattooing.

Kat Von D: I got into tattooing about the same time I started tattooing, which was fourteen years old, just hanging out with a lot of kids in the punk rock scene, you know? All my friends had tattoos and being naturally inclined to the art, it was just something that kinda naturally came.

Where was this?

This was in San Bernardino. That's where I was kinda raised.

Inland Empire.

Yeah, yeah. I was born in Mexico and I came to America when I was about four years old.

And you got tattooed at fourteen?

Yeah, and it was all homemade stuff and that's kinda how I started. Just like tattooing a lot of gangsters and shit like that, and the punk rock kids. And then I got into my first tattoo shop when I was sixteen. That was in San Bernardino at Sin City Tattoo. And I worked there for about a year and a half or so and then moved to Pasadena.

Was it mostly machines or were you guys doing needles and india ink?

No, we had rigged up machines to the whole cassette player motor and all that stuff. It was all guitar string that we'd filed down and all that stuff. Sometimes we'd get fancy and make a foot pedal, but for the most part it was just hooked up to a battery.

And then you came to L.A.?

Yeah, then I came to L.A. I worked at a few shops before I started working out at High Voltage in Hollywood, which is my favorite shop that I've ever worked at.

And you're here permanently now?

Yeah, pretty much. I want to be here for a long time.

How many people think that you're in Miami?

A lot of people think that I'm in Miami just because of the show [*Miami Ink*], and people just assume that I live there. But I would actually never ever live there. The only reason I'm there is because they pay me.

And how did you get into your specialty doing the black and gray?

You know, as a kid I would always draw portraits of my family members, so I think I've always been drawn to realism. So when I started tattooing, I tried to do my realistic take on everything. So, even with traditional stuff, I'd always shade it out too much and kinda lose that whole traditional effect to it. But now I pretty much just stick to fine-line black and gray. I don't really do that much color nowadays. I mean on my friends I'll do it, but I want to focus on something and just stick to it.

Do you see yourself continuing with your other work you're doing? Which is, like, on calendars and your—

Yeah, you know, because of the show and the success of it, I've been able to launch a merchandise store, I guess you could call it, where I sell, like, tattoo-influenced clothing and calendars and shot glasses and bells and things like that. I mean, I eventually plan on expanding and actually doing, like, a legit clothing line, so I think that might be a plan for the future. But I don't know. I'm just trying to kinda build my little empire right now.

And how did you feel about getting in so young, because you were so young coming into the scene—especially as a woman?

Yeah, I'm really grateful I got into tattooing as young as I did because I feel like I was able to learn more at such a young age. And I have a lot of years ahead of me now because of it. But it was

tough at the same time, you know? I didn't really understand what I was getting into when I got into it. I just was like, this is something I want to do—I love it. But then you start realizing all the politics, and all the tattoo drama that comes along with it, which I've tried my hardest to stay out of. But it's definitely a lifestyle and it's something that I'm pretty loyal to.

Do you ever get people who ask you to do stuff you just don't want to do?

I think at this point in my career I can pick and choose what I want to do, so out of all the requests I get I just kinda pick the ones I want to do. I just feel like, you know, I have a certain amount of years to my tattoo life and there's a certain amount of tattoos that I can do in that time. And I'd rather focus on the things that I want to perfect. I want to be better than what I am right now. So it's like, I'd rather just focus on doing the portraits and the realism and the black and gray.

When I was in Japan getting tattooed, I saw Horiyoshi Sensei doing this insect on this girl's back—like an American dragonfly—and when I asked him about it, he said, "It's what she wanted." It's just so weird to go to Japan to have him do something that wasn't his style.

Yeah, I'm not in any way trying to say that I'm better than certain styles. I just feel like I'm good at what I do and I know my limits. Like I would never attempt doing a Japanese sleeve because my brain doesn't think the same way. And I would never want somebody to be unhappy with what they get. I'd be much happier referring them to somebody who specializes in what they love, you know?

You have a favorite piece on you?
I think my favorite tattoo that I have is the portrait of my father on my right arm. It was done by Tim Hendrix. My father has always been my hero growing up and still is. I can always look down at my arm and look at my dad. And he loves the tattoo, so it's cool.

What brought you guys here from Mexico?
My brother, my sister, and I were born in Monterrey in Nuevo León, Mexico. But my family is actually from Argentina. My parents were missionaries for the church at the time and they were going to school in Mexico and doing missionary work and whatnot. And the three of us were born and then we came to America.

What do you think about how tattoos have changed in terms of being so much more prevalent now than when you were growing up?
Well, you know, especially with the popularity of these TV shows and things like that, it has definitely opened people's minds up to tattooing. Nowadays you've got soccer moms and people that normally wouldn't be into tattooing tuning in. Even though they might not necessarily get a sleeve or get tattooed, they can now appreciate it and understand why people get tattooed. So I think that in a way it's really nice and at the same time, I kinda liked, you know, feeling punk rock and being the only—

More underground.
Yeah. You know, being the only person—the only girl—with her face tattooed or having full sleeves, you know? But at the same time, it was still a pain in the ass. Even like five years ago it was so different . . . going to malls or going to a Christian Dior store, you don't get the same respect that you get now. People are way more open-minded to it.

So you had problems when you were a kid?
Well sure. You know, I was young and had visible tattoos and living in the Inland Empire wasn't like—it wasn't Hollywood.

[laughs] I♂ . . . I was born in ♂ontana.
Oh yeah! So you know all about it.

It's so different than just—
I think, you know, once like, Britney Spears and Christina Aguilera and Angelina Jolie started getting heavily tattooed . . . those are the people that launched the popularity before these shows appeared. I think these shows just kind of exploded it for the rest of them.

How about face tattoos? Anyone ever copy you?
You know, I saw a few girls that got it and it really bums me out because like—obviously, I'm not the first person to get a star on your face. But, like the way that I got the stars on my face was something to be an individual, like the rest of my tattoos. It was something that meant something to me and I liked the way it looked on me. And so when you see other girls doing it—and a lot of girls, whether they're copying my style or what-ever—you have to take it as a compliment. But if it was up to me, I wouldn't want them to do it.

Right.
I mean, having your face tattooed is a really big step and it's not something that I promote, you know? It's like, I'm a tattooer. It's what I do for a living. I feel comfortable in my skin. But some people at a really young age, they just go crazy. And it's like, dude, you still gotta get a job and you still gotta function in society.

The first ones I saw were the stars and I have seen people try to copy that.
Yeah, yeah. It's a bummer . . . and I mean, in the same sense it's like, everything's been done, you know? Tattooing's been around forever and we're just regurgitating different styles and either improving them or taking our own take on it.

Exactly.
But, you know, it does suck when somebody—I would never go into a tattoo shop and show them a magazine and go, "This is what I want."

Exactly _this_.
Which is what people do.

Any last advice for people thinking about getting their tattoos?
Just do your research. I think there's tons of amazing artists out there. You don't have to stick to one person. There's a lot of people out there that you could check out their work and their styles before just going into any shop to get just any random tattoo.

One Day... Chris Garver and I were working together — we ended up finishing sooner than we expected —

So on a whim... we decided to tattoo my neck. Garver smoked some pot, drew on my neck with a pen, and the next thing you know — BAM! I got my neck tattooed!

Everybody has special
meanings for their tattoos.
I don't.
I just like japanese stuff.

Plethora

Basket

Grey

Rain

Terrible

Pretty

Lovely

Lavender

Spectacular

The Number of words That caught My eye after I Decided I was Getting a word Search. I Really Love The way Lettering Looks on The Human Body, But I Felt uncomfortable Puting a quote on My Body Because I Feel The Things I Put under My skin should Be Mine. I started The List of words on Orange Sticky Notes. There were alot of Three Letter words That were unintended showing up, such as Fat, and Cat.

I have a japanese
mom who lives in Hawaii
and HATES my tattoos...
every time i go home, she
makes me wear long
sleeved shirts in 85° hawaiian
heat so she doesn't have
to see them.

PAin theRApy

E-3, L-12, BAt-7

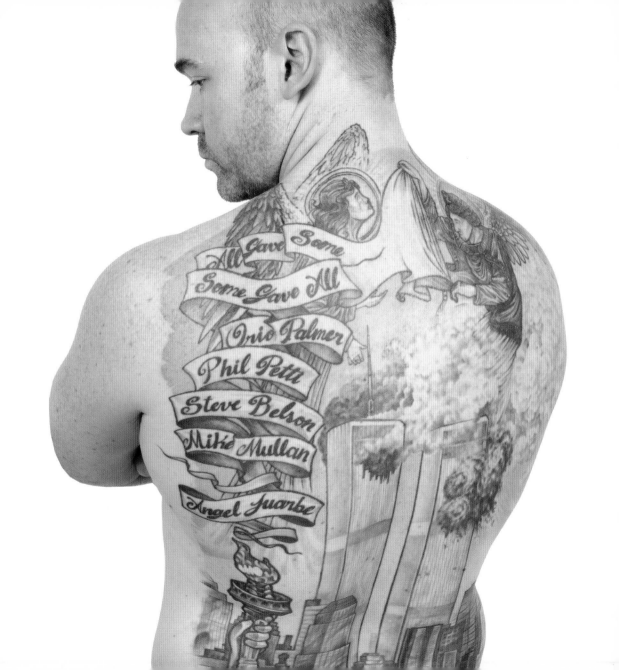

Mom hates tatoos of any kind because of her polish heritage. In Poland, as a child, she was forced to visit the concentration camps before they had been cleaned up or altered—and been deadly effected by the way people had been "branded". Tatoo's reminded her of this. Since she was catholic, I figured if I picked a random name from the Bible, it wouldn't be quite as bad. It was self-made when I was 15 by a sharpened guitar string and indian ink.

My Lucky Wrench, one day sitting in
my car with wife and daughter in pollo
Loco. i came to an Idea of a wrench
on my neck for Luck. So cAlled my budy
up. Late night that day we were on the table
getting dun. Now I have the problem every one
thinks its a penis -. not Finish yet.

GETTING A TATTOO HURTS, BUT SOMETIMES THE REASON BEHIND WHY YOU GET A TATTOO IS EVEN MORE PAINFUL... EX-LOVER, THAT BAND YOU THOUGHT WAS SO AWESOME AT THE TIME, SPRING BREAK MADNESS CAN ALL ADD UP TO REGRETS. BUT WHAT ABOUT THE LOSS OF A LOVED PERSON? YOU HAVE ~~HAD~~ NO CONTROL AND THAT MAY BE YOUR ONLY REGRET. I HAVE NO REGRETS, BUT I WILL FOREVER HAVE MY REMINDER OF HOW I FELT WHEN MY LIFE CHANGED.

My tattoo means "peace" in french. I have struggled with severe anorexia reaching a weight of 86 pounds at a height of 5'9. I decided/was forced to get help at a hospital for 2 long months and slowly was able to recover. I am now accepting of my # flaws and at peace mind, body and spirit. It is written in french because french women are thin.

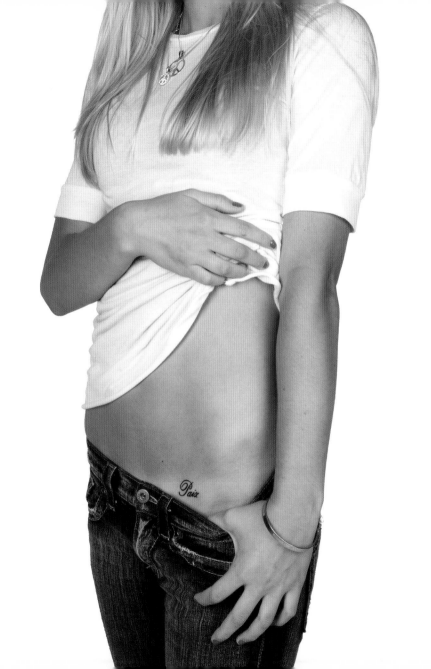

IN Honor of my GRANDparents.
TRADITIONAL SAMOA SEAL. BITS
AND pieces from my GRANDFATHERS
"PEA"! REPPING FOR ALL THE USO'S

H.B./KAVA.
JOE SAMATUA

THIS TATTOO TOOK TWICE AS LONG TO FINISH BECAUSE ① I AM A BIG BABY AND ② IT'S ON A "THIN-SKINNED" AREA OF THE BODY. THIN-SKINNED. NOW THAT I AM FULLY ENSCONDED IN MY OPRAH-BEFORE-THE-LAST-DIET-STUCK PERIOD OF MIDDLE AGE DOM, I LOVE THE FACT THAT I HAVE SUCH A BEAUTIFULLY DECORATED "THIN-SKINNED AREA OF THE BODY." EVERY ONCE IN A WHILE I SEE A FLASH OF TATT AND I SMILE. THIN SKIN REMAINS ON A BODY THAT HAS BECOME ALL FLESHY CURVES AND VOLUPTOUS THIGHS.

FYI

THE CENTRAL FIGURE IS A "NKYINKYIM" FROM WEST AFRICA. IT SYMBOLIZES DYNAMISM AND VERSATILITY. IT'S SURROUNDED BY STARS FROM A MIRO PAINTING WITH A FRAME TAKEN FROM A MEXICAN WOOD PRINT. HEREIN LIES A TALE FOR ANOTHER DAY.

~~PRIDE~~ GOT MY PRIDE TRIANGLE AT
AGE 19. I WAS AT A POINT IN MY
LIFE THAT I WAS COMFORTABLE WITH
WHO I AM. MOM WASN'T VERY HAPPY!!
BUT SHE GOT USED TO IT AND
MY MANY GIRLFRIENDS THAT CAME
~~WITH~~ WITH IT!!

V-Vay

My first tattoo was an iron cross
that I did myself when I was 12.
I work in the morgue as a file clerk.
I type up toe tags + files for the coroners office
I love going to school for Criminal Justice
so I can be a police officer.
I want to be a CSI for the LAPD.
I'm also in a band singing for my supper,

    It's Not the things That most men fear,
that make me most afraid;
But skies that Burn too brightly Blue;
And tunes to sweetly played.

                        - 7th grade poetry class.

I'VE ALWAYS HAD A FASCINATION WITH OLD PISTOLS. THE PEACEMAKER SEEMED PERFECT FOR AN ALMOST IRONIC STATEMENT. THE SKULLS REPRESENT DEATH OF COURSE.

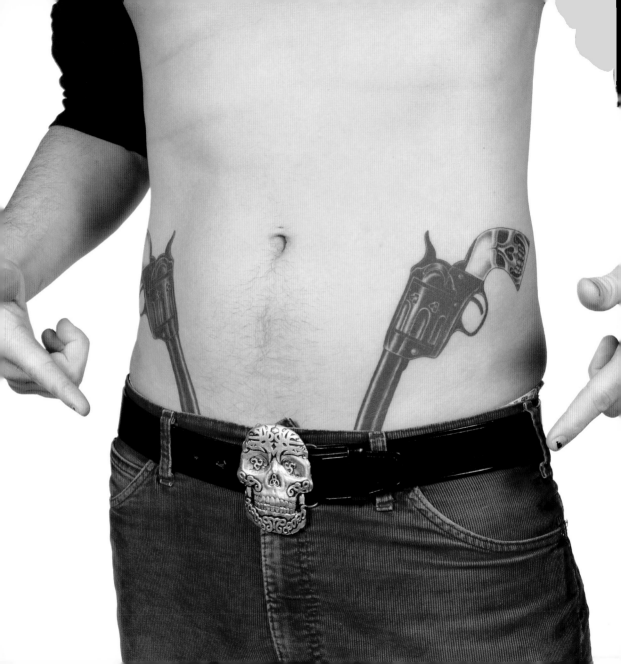

I loved my cherry tattoo
when I got it. It was
there to cover up another
one that didnt come out
right. And then I got
pregnant & it stretched out
ending up bigger (way bigger)
than it was...
My new tattoos surround the
cherries, though. The most
beautiful stretch marks from my
unborn baby, isnt he
gorgeous?

I got my tattoo in LaCrosse, Wisconsin Before ll got deployed to IRAQ. I love being a paratrooper. In my arm to represent strength and chest close to my heart. I love my country believe in it and willing to give my life, as I am sworn to do.

SSG Zulueta

It started with my wife's name on my
arm in 1966.
My mother told me before I went in
the service to never get a tattoo,
I disobeyed.

This is an infinity symbol.

basically.

Never get a tat by someone whom you refer to as "someguy". When trying to decide on what to get, he asked me who my favorite band was. It was Alice in Chains. He pulled out the CD and went with it. He went so deep, it scarred up. My tattoo is so raised that it is like brialle. Tattoos for the blind.

I love ♥s,

but I don't

trust 'em ...

Interview with Brittany Farmer

Kip Fulbeck: Tell me how you decided to get a tattoo.

Brittany Farmer: I decided I wanted a tattoo probably in high school. It wasn't a really big deal because most of my family has tattoos. And then I was thinking about it a lot when I came to college.

How old are you now?

I'm nineteen. [laughs] And I got it on my nineteenth birthday. The first go-around I had some elaborate design like an orchid and this whole thing and I had this tattoo artist draw it up for me. And then I made the appointment and chickened out at the last minute and I didn't call him—mostly because I didn't want to be tattooed at a place called Precious Slut. [laughs] And also because, I think it was kind of one of those things where I knew in my gut it wasn't the right one to have. I didn't have that "for sure" feeling that I think you should have before you go into something that's going to last forever.

So what happened?

So I didn't get it done. I chickened out. And then about six months later, I was still thinking about it and I really wanted to get something done. And at the time I was going through a lot changes with myself, just as far as my Christian identity is concerned. Before, I was very by the book . . . typical youth group, non-Catholic; people will teach you about the Bible and Christian life—I would go by that. And then all of sudden I had all these questions and all these doubts.

Like what?

I had a lot of trouble with . . . the way they teach is very in a box and I never felt like I really belonged in the world they were trying to create—where women are traditionally, they're docile and obedient to their husbands. It was mostly being a female, I think. Just second best to the male gender. I just didn't feel like that was God's intent for women to be second best. And that really started the ball rolling . . . and also with homosexuality and things like this where people justify telling people that they're going to go to hell for certain behavior when the entire rest of the Bible preaches about love and forgiveness and acceptance.

And how did that bring you to get a tattoo?

I wanted something that would signify what I knew for sure. And that was that there is a God. And for me, you know, it's the God of the Bible and that God is always with me and cares about me. And that's one thing I knew for absolute sure and that I still know. So, I just kind of wanted to remind myself of that in this whole world of change. That there is something permanent for me, right there. So I was flipping through images, Christian iconography, on the Web. And I didn't want to get a cross because it seems kind of cliché. I wanted something a little more unique, a little more personal. And I just found this symbol of the triangle representing the Trinity and the circle representing eternity. And I decided that that would be something nice and simple and clean and kind of like me.

How did your family feel?

My mom did not want me to get a tattoo until I was about thirty-five years old, so I'd know I'd like it the rest of my life.

But you got it at nineteen?

It was sort of my first act of rebellion. Although, I guess it's kind of a weak rebellion, rebelling toward a tattoo about God. [laughs] That's okay. It's me. So I went down, I didn't tell her I was gonna get it. I didn't tell anybody, actually. I took two of my roommates and we went down to the tattoo parlor called Custom Ink, this time, which was a little bit more acceptable to me. And he did the tattoo. And it hurt! Just about as much as a Brazilian bikini wax, I'd say. They're about on the same level of pain for me. [laughs] And I was just really happy with it and it was really one of the first things I'd done that I didn't care what other people thought about it. You know, my mom told me "wait," and my dad probably didn't really care, and my boyfriend said, "Are you sure you really want to get a tattoo on your foot?" because of this and this and this. And it was just one of those things where I knew I wanted it, so I did it for me. No questions asked type of thing.

How do you feel about all the tattoos going around with your college friends . . . all the tattoos that you see everywhere?

I think a lot of tattoos that girls are getting especially—and guys, too—they'll end up thinking they're dumb later in life. Getting tattoos is really trendy on the college campus. And I think that people just want a tattoo and don't want to think about what it means. So people end up with punk rock stars on their wrists or a NorCal symbol huge across their back. And it might be meaning-ful for some people, but when you see twenty-five of them walking down the street, you know not everybody is that connected to that thing. So when you go into the tattoo parlors and flip through all the stock images and you can name fifteen people that have it, I think it kind of loses its relevance in a way. I think it's something that should say something about you, permanently, say something about who you are—not just something you liked at a certain age.

What would happen if all of a sudden you saw a whole bunch of college girls all getting the same tattoo you have now?
Um . . . it wouldn't really bother me because I know what it means for me.

What if you started a trend and you were the first one and then all of a sudden fifty people have yours?
[laughs] If all of a sudden people had mine, I . . . you know, it wouldn't really bother me if people really connected with it. It would bother me if people, all of a sudden it became an image where it's seen everywhere and then people would come up to me and go, "Oh, so you're just another person with that tattoo." That would bother me. Because I'd have to be on the defensive about it and explain everything. But if I started a trend, that would be flattering. [laughs]

How do you feel about tattoos on men?
I like tattoos on guys or don't. I think it depends on if it fits the person, then it's nice. It can complement the person. But, you know, the armband, tribal tattoo that everybody got in the early '90s, like Nick Lachey–type tattoo, I don't like those,

because they just seem, they seem fake. They seem just trendy. Just like you went out with your bros and you all bleached your hair and got an armband tattoo. But, like, my cousin has this full-body tattoo. And for him it fits his entire personality, and every tattoo, he sat down with the artist and helped design it. And he did a lot of the sketches himself. So for that, it's meaningful and it's him. If you see his tattoos it says a lot about who he is. So I like those ones.

Have you ever had any of your girlfriends ask you for advice on their tattoos?
Right after I got my foot tattoo my roommate now decided that she wanted to get one, um, on her foot! But she didn't want to do it in the same place, you know, as a me type of thing. And she wanted to get something a little bit different. So she just kind of asked me about how much did it hurt or "What do you think about this?" showing me things. But I think she was talking about it a little bit before I did it and then as soon as I did it she was like, "All right, I want to do it."

What happened?
She went and got it done. It's right on the side of her foot and not on the top.

Would she have gotten it on her foot if you didn't?
Um . . . she was looking for a place, I think the same as me—she was looking for a place that was kind of appropriate. For example, like you don't want to get a cross on your ass because it's just kind of odd. I mean, if you want to you can. But she was looking for sort of that appropriate place and I think she likes mine. I'm not the only person in the world with a foot tattoo, so I'm not gonna take credit for that.

Any advice for people who are looking at tattoos?
I'd say, obviously think about it, not that I thought about it a certain amount of time. But the most important thing is, I think, go with your gut. Because if you see something, you know you love it. Give it a couple of days to make sure that feeling still sticks or, you know, however long you want to wait. For me it was just a couple of days. But if you know it, then do it and you'll probably be happy with it. But if you have any inkling of, you know, "I'm not certain about this," I would say just—however embarrassing it might be that you don't show your face at Precious Slut anymore—don't do it! You're going to regret it when you're eighty years old with a tattoo you don't like.

Anything to say to your tattooer who's waiting for you at Precious Slut?
[laughs] Your sketch was beautiful. But it just wasn't for me and I wish you'd change the name of your store. Well, for people like me, anyway! [laughs]

The tattoo symbolizes the eternal trinity (Father, Son, Holy Spirit) and marks the first thing I've ever done strictly for myself, without regard for other opinions. After starting college, I went through a lot of changes with my Christian identity trying to make sense of tradition vs universal truths. I decided that the one thing I knew for sure was that there is a God and that God is with me no matter what changes I may go through.

My tattoos are by Ed Hardy. He is the greatest. I'm so proud of them but I also want them to stay perfect forever so I don't show them off a lot. They never see the sun and I only view them by candlelight. Now I want more more more...

tattooing my face was the best way I could
say fuck yor to everyone who judges people
for what they look like and not who they
are or what they believe in.

*Tattoos are an expression of who you are. My Lion is a manifestation of my strength & will power (& sometimes my "wild") side. I knew basically what I wanted for years, but I just couldn't find something that fit me. Now I have it... along with an amazing boy-friend (a perfect fit.) Chris has been the incarnation of strength for me this past year, so it's only fitting that he took me to Taki-San & stayed with me while I got my ink done... like I said "perfect fit"!

*We've had a crazy year... dealt with a lot of pain. It's ended in beauty, though - just like a tattoo. Even the painful moments have been precious and full of value. I'm lucky.

KEEP TATTOOING POWERFUL —

A STATEMENT è A REMINDER .

Old sttye tattoo of the 60's. Spider + a
peace sign. Done the old way (homemade)
A fine sewing needle with fine thread wrapped
on the tip dipped in sterile Indian Ink.
I was around 14 @ the time + I just
happened to. be facinated with spider's
+ the peace movement of the 60's.
I was also a very lanky kid at for
during my early teen year + some
of my friends used to at time call
me spider. This went on through
my early years as well.

Oh The Memories.

I ♡ ART
I ♡ EXPRESSION
I ♡ THE HUMAN BODY
I ♡ TATTOOS
I ♡ PINK MOHAWKS
I ♡ ORCHIDS
♡♡♡
I ♡ ALL OF THE ABOVE
:)

I've wanted tattoos since I was a little
girl... They make me happy.

~~[scribbled out]~~ ~~[scribbled out]~~
~~[scribbled out]~~.

The butterflies were my first on
my arm and probably and my favorite.
I can't wait to be grandma with
tattoos. . . . .

I've always loved the idea of tattoos — having something mean so much that you would permanently ink it on your body forever. For me, it took years to understand and ultimately celebrate who and what I actually was. The moment I came to that realization, I wanted a constant reminder of both the pain and the beauty of being hapa.

HI: MY NAME IS MARCUS AND NEED TO WORKOUT MORE!

I WANT TO PLAY! FOOTBALL!,

RIGHT NOW!

I got tatted at age 19

I STARTED GETTING TATTOOS WHEN
I WAS ~~21~~ 15, Needle And INDiAN INK,
WE EVEN BURNED Some PLASTIC SPOONS
AND mixed It with SHAMPOO TO
MAKE INK! THAt WAS FOR A
MOTOR heAd TATTOO oN mY WRIST, 25
yEArS)ATer i still get 1 ABouT
EverY TWO yEArS, The ANchor is
FOR The NAUY BASE mY mom AND I
WErE BoTh BornAT, "NAUY BrAT"

TxCxBx OxOxCx

CAPT SEAN "DOE" WHEELER

SUN TRASH

私は日本で刺青師をしています。
この仕事を始めてから約14年
になります。
14年が長いのか短いのかわか
らないけど、これからも
この仕事を続けられれば
幸せですね。

This is easy. I was 13. My pop was a Jersey City Cop. He took me for my 1st tat From that moment on tats have been a part of my everyday life. People that dont have tats are pussies. A tat is a way of life not a trendy pass time Fuk

~~A lot of my tattoos are taken~~ ~~from famous~~ I'm not very balanced. "Fifty" was my first stuffed animal. ~~I named him~~ for 50 dollars. Obscure ~~references that~~ tell a life story, ideology, methodology never entered my mind. ~~[scribble]~~ one time a guy said "there̶s̶ ̶a̶ naked midget on your back". I told him, "you don't have to whisper". There's always a new tattoo in my head.

You Can't walk
With out Your legs.

This tattoo is in honor of the
Marines in my platoon who
were killed in 'Husaybah, Iraq.

I told one of them I would get a
tattoo in his honor if he was
killed. He died on April 17, 2004.

"Never Forget" has two
meanings —
1. For me to never forget my
fallen brothers;

2. For all those who see this
tattoo to never forget the
cost of War.

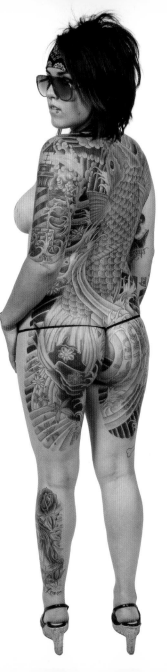

I bare pieces of my
heart.   I am an art
collecter

If you go back far enough, the name Velasquez comes from Belasco, which means 'Son of Raven' in Basque . . . . or at least I hope it does.

Yeah, I know, damn she is hella white... hey but I got to represent my self as the whitest half Chinese girl around!!! HAPA PRIDE! I have my light colored hair, so I used to shave my eyebrows off and draw them on with eye liner. Well one day I forgot to draw my damn eyebrows on. I looked in the mirror in the car before work and then..... damn, I had no eyebrows, I reached down for the crayola marker and drew them on. At that I knew I had to get these damn things put on my damn face for life. :) Gina 陈

I woke up one morning at the Hyatt on Sunset, had breakfast with the band and left without telling where I was going. Lyle Tuttle was across the street and I went over for a little ink. I promised myself there would only be one.

I Kept The Promise

Interview with Oliver Peck

Kip Fulbeck: Tell me how you got into tattooing.
Oliver Peck: I guess pretty much the same as everybody does, just fascinated by art as a kid. I was always drawing and once you get old enough you start drawing yourself and getting bubble-gum-machine tattoos when you're a kid. I grew up in Fort Worth, Texas, which is kind of not the big city life at all. I mean, it's a city—it's a downtown—but it's kinda like a small-town city. There's not much diversity there at all. It's pretty much rednecks. And the only tattooed people I ever saw were people that my mom would steer me away from. It's like, you see a biker, or some gangster, or a convict-looking guy with tattoos and I was always like, "Man, that's awesome. That's what I want. When I get old I'm gonna get tattoos."

And this was the '70s?
Yeah, this is early, like when I was, like, five, six, seven, eight, nine, ten . . . you know, '70s, late '70s. And then, once I got into high school, got on drugs, whatnot, met some people who knew how to make homemade tattoo machines, I just started tattooing on myself, started tattooing on friends.

What was the first one you did?
First one I did on myself was without a machine. Just a straight loose needle and some ink. I hand-poked on my ankles a moon and a star. Later I came to find out that it was a Muslim symbol.

Yeah. [laughs]
[laughs] But at the time in my teenage years, it was actually a skateboard graphic from Todd Swank. And it was just, he just had a moon and a star, and I was just like—at the actual night that it came to be that I got that tattoo, that sticker was there and it was a simple, easy design. There was not that much thought put into what my first tattoo was gonna be. It was just, "I want something. Okay, how about that?"

How old were you?
I might have been sixteen. Either sixteen or seventeen. It was in the summer . . . eighth-grade summer, ninth-grade summer, tenth-grade summer. Something like that.

So you cut your chops in Fort Worth?
Yeah, then I started tattooing more friends and made some homemade tattoo machines. And then I ended up moving to Dallas after high school and actually purchased some legitimate

tattoo equipment and was tattooing out of my house. And then, just got a job at a shop from some referral. Some guy I tattooed went in the shop and they said, "Who did that?" "Oh, this kid." I went and got a job there pretty much. It was really, you know, just a little-budget, no-good little tattoo shop. And I worked there for a few months and started hanging out at another shop in town called Paradise that Richard Stell owned at the time. And he was like a long-term, old-school veteran tattooer in Texas that was really badass. I started hanging out over there and made friends with him and the guys that work there and one day he just asked me if I wanted to learn how to tattoo.

Really? Just took you on like that?

Hell, he was like, "You want to learn how to tattoo?" And I was like, "Fuck yeah!" He's like, "Well, come work over here and start all over and we'll teach you how to tattoo." So that's what I did. I worked there for about five years and really learned to tattoo and built a clientele in Dallas . . . a few years after that me and some partners opened up Elm Street Tattoo in Dallas, which I've been there for going on eleven years now.

How much time you spending out here now?

Just within the last five or six years I've started working in L.A. and California. First was working in Orange County at Classic Tattoo with Eric Maaske. And he was the person who brought me out to California. Because I met him on some road trips and he really changed my life and changed my tattooing and brought me into the style of tattooing that I do now, which is old-school, traditional, American, whatever you want to call it. I worked for him at his shop and I was going back and forth between Dallas and Orange County until he died two years ago. And then I started working in L.A. at True Tattoo. So now I've evolved to where I'm in L.A. half the time. I do two weeks in Dallas, two weeks in L.A. every month.

What do you think about the resurgence in traditional American style now?

A few years ago, the whole classic tattoo American thing—like the old-school tattooing thing—has really become a big buzz with clothing companies and refrigerator magnets, and Sailor Jerry Rum and Ed Hardy Clothing Company. It's good and it's bad. Now you have a lot more people getting the style of tattoos that I like, but then you also have people that you don't like getting that style of tattoos. So it's like, there's always good with the bad. There's people that are getting it because they love it and people that are getting it just because somebody else got it. It's like, you know, you miss the old days when people were original. Tattooing has really gotten so crazy. It's so popular. I mean now there's, like, crazy fads and trends in tattooing. Like, there'll go years where everybody gets a tribal armband and then years where everybody gets a swallow and then years when everybody wants a Japanese koi fish. You know, when I was early tattooing, every college girl got a butterfly on her butt or a dolphin on her ankle. Early '90s, I bet there was more dolphins tattooed than anything else for, like, three years straight. Every sorority girl had a dolphin on her ankle.

And then mid-'90s was the tribal?

Yeah. Every dude had a tribal armband and every girl had a little tribal shape on her lower back. It's weird because tattooing originally, I mean the way most people get into tattooing is because they want it, you know, it's the desire for art and a desire for individuality. And now it's almost become the exact opposite of both. Now it's like, it's *not* about the art and it's *not* about the individual. It's about picking whatever's hip and getting whatever whoever else got. So, it's like, it's totally opposite of what it used to be.

What do you think is going to happen over time with that?

Who knows? A lot of people say that tattooing is this growing fad and it could crash at any minute, but they forget to remember that all these people have these tats and they're stuck with them.

Forty million people.

All these people. You can't stop something like that. You can't—it's not something that can be forgotten because every new kid that turns eighteen every day is gonna see someone with a tattoo—whether that person they saw still likes their tattoo or not, that eighteen-year-old kid is still gonna be influenced by it. There's no turning around. You can't erase it. And even though people are all, "Oh, people are getting their tattoos removed," that's like, there's, it's still not possible to remove . . . I mean maybe the technology'll get better to where they can just walk in and [snaps finger] zap your tattoo off painlessly. But until that happens, it's not—

I can't imagine getting this off. I mean how much, how long it would take?

Yeah, anybody that's heavily tattooed has no hope—

You could just blacken your arms out at some point.

People do that, too. And that's still going to influence the next generation to get tattooed. No matter what, no matter how much you discourage young kids not to do heroin, every year there's more heroin junkies on the street. I think the main thing that's gonna probably try to hurt tattooing is the legal aspect. Because now they're coming into health issues and the health department's coming in and they're gonna start registering and monitoring the uses of the inks and everything. Like the FDA approves food, they're gonna try to approve the inks. And the inks we use—they're safe, comparably speaking. But they're not medically proven safe by any medical standard to have a product shoved underneath your skin.

There's no research on it.

Yeah and no. The research they're doing now is showing that the ink is not—they're considering it not safe. Now they put out warning labels on—I think they're gonna start putting warning labels on tattoo shop doors saying it could be hazardous to your health.

Really? They're not talking about hep and communicables?

No, they're talking about the ink filtering through, like when your body filters it out. They're finding people that are old have clogged-up ink in their livers and in their organs and stuff. I mean, whatever. I mean, people are still gonna do it. You put a skull and crossbones on a cigarette pack and people still buy it. People are gonna still do it, whether they say it's safe or not.

Of course.

I mean, it's made it through the scare of disease in the '80s. In the '80s and early '90s there was a big scare of disease transferred from tattooing and people are getting tattooed more now than ever. So who knows?

What's your advice for people thinking about getting tattooed?

I think that there's a fine line to be crossed between thinking about what tattoo to get and thinking too much about what tattoo to get. If you're the kind of person that's gonna think too much about what to get, then maybe you shouldn't get it. You know . . . the kind of people that do tons of research and the kind of people who spend months and months deciding on one little factor of their one little, small tattoo that

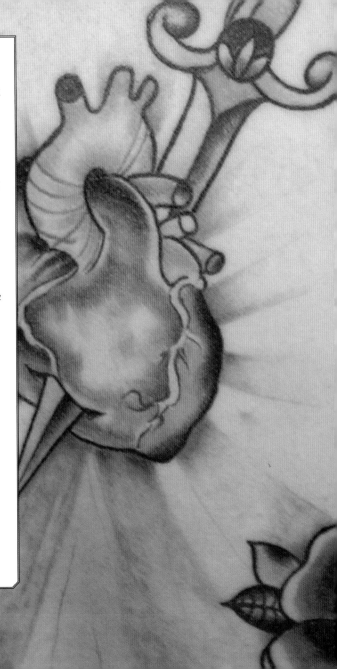

they're gonna get—those are the people who regret their tattoo. The people that just come in and be like, "I want this. I want that. I want to get a tattoo because I love tattoos because I love art" . . . those people, like me, they don't regret their tattoos. Regardless of whether they were done well or done bad or faded or old or shiny or new. It's like, if you're getting tattooed, you should get tattooed because you love tattoos. End of the story. You know? That's it. People that try and find other reasons to get tattoos, they're just . . . it's a false hope and they're building themselves up to be let down later because it's still just gonna be a tattoo and it's still gonna be old some day and it's still gonna be . . .

It won't be trendy at some point.
Yeah.

It'll change.
I mean, whatever you get . . . if you get it because it's hip, it's not gonna be hip some day, you know? If you get it because you love it, then you're set. You got nothing to worry about.

I started getting tattooed IN
a period oF my LIFE where all
my decisions were MADE under
a Heavy L.S.D. iNFluence, and
its like oNce you get started
your Just another ~~Loser~~ Loser
with a Few tats iF you Quit
Then, So Here I am a real
WiNNer at the game oF LIFE.

P.S. IF youve neve done L.S.D
        DO IT
And if youvre iN school
        DROP OUT   Oliver Peck

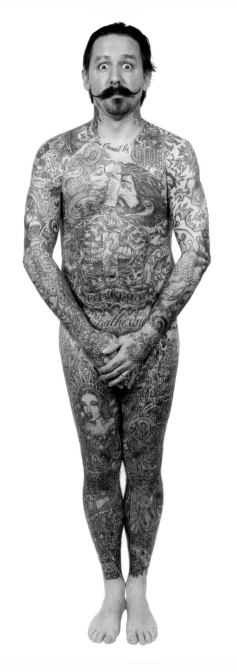

私は ~~本~~ すえひろ ~~まさ~~ まるお
大好きです。とても かっこいいですね。
じ ~~さ~~ 魚 が 好きです。

My tattoo was inspired
by a manga by Suehiro
Maruo. I love ero-grotesque
art. Yeah. My artist was
very hesitant to do it at first
but I think he was very happy
to do it after he saw the out-
line on my back. — I have
never taken my shirt off for
so many strangers in my
life. — Beth. Sorry for
my terrible Japanese grammar.

MARY Got MY NAME "Scott's"
Below Her... um Belly Button
while I WAS in JAIL -
8 years Ago AS AN EXpression
of Loyalty. GETTING HER
FACE TATTooed on MY ArM
is the same sHow of
DEVOTION. (Besides the Fact
that I JUST like Being
reminded of How Beautiful
SHe is)

Take this Shit off no

More husband no move

Tattoo!!

Cover this Shit up!!!.

TATTOO IS my Family
Mom, Dad, ME, ¿ Bro
Tattoo My

Sulu'Ape AISEA

I have 2 kids and I have been a
stay at home Mon the entire time.
My tattoo on my side did not get
ruined during my pregnancies
Thank God. I was heavily tattooed
before I married my husband
Ryan Groebler who is currently ~~doing~~
~~~~ working on my side piece. Its very
romantic. I think its funny that
the only time I get a baby sitter is
to get tattoed.

— SAROJ

MY BUDDY THOMAS GOT A TATTOO
MACHINE FOR CHRISTMAS. HE NEVER
DONE A TATTOO IN HIS LIFE SO I LET
HIM TRY IT OUT ON MY FEET. THE
FIRST ONE WAS THE SABBATH ON
MY LEG. THE NEXT DAY I WANTED
MORE SO WE WERE THINKIN WHAT
WOULD BE GOOD ON MY TOES. I LOVE
BACON FIT PERFECT SO IT WAS A GO.
A COUPLE WEEKS LATER HE DID
BART SIMPSON "EL BARTO WAS HERE"
AT ABOUT 3:00 IN THE MORNING.
I LOVE THE SIMPSONS TOO SO I HAD
TO GET IT ON MY ARM. THANKS
FUNDILLO BREATH. NSK 4LIFE
NSK KRUE RICHIE BELTON

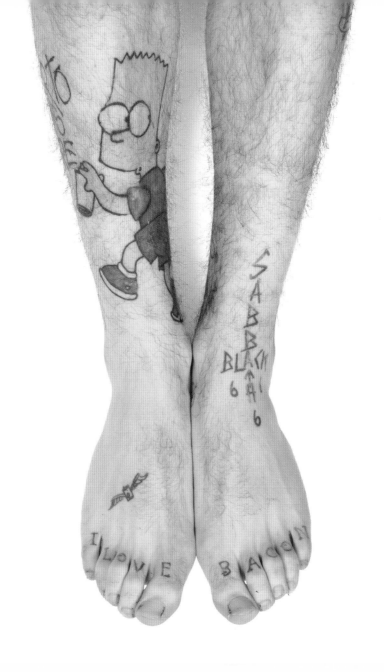

Who doesn't wanna be like Superman? Everyone wants to be like him. He's the original superhero. ...And he can fly!

It's the 1st
tattoo I got in Japan.
Having it done by
Horijosh III was pretty
sweet! He's an awesome
guy .... he tattooed me
on his day off. It's the
first hand poke tattoo I
have that wasn't done
with needle and thread

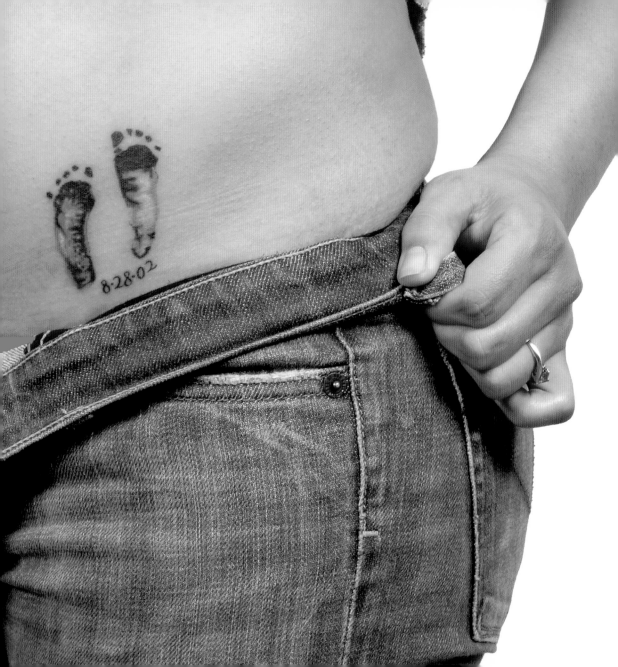

My First tattoo is baby Foot prints with the due date below it. I was 18yrs. old and had an abortion, although I was young I know I made a mistake. So the reason why I got it done is because it means alot to ~~be~~ me...

Always

♥ 5·3·6 ♥

I do HAVE THem BECUSE
I AM FigHTeR

Horiyuki

彫ゆき

廠ゆき

My parents converted to the Mormon church when I was young. I got baptized at 8 and came out when I was 16. Being gay led to a rapid departure from the church and my parent's house. I got this tattoo when I was 17 or 18 on a drunken whim, I can't remember exactly... It was a crazy time of rebellion and exploration.

-Johnny Z.

My tattoo of Our Lady of Guadalupe is very important to me. I was a very young mother, and now I have 3 children who are everything to me. I have changed a lot in the last 14 years as a mother and as a person. The Virgin is who I pray to to have more patience and to be a better mother to my children, I am also Catholic. She is the best mother that I know of.

I got this tattoo when I turned 30. Being disabled and a person of short stature (midget to y'alls) I always felt out of place. I finally came to a point in my life where I said "fuck it" + decided to be 'me'. I dyed my hair funky colors, got a tattoo + started to do adult modeling. I run a site called 6impsgonewild.com it's to show the world that us 6imp/midget chicks are hot + sexy too. My tattoo is a representation of my change + freedom of expression. I feel that life is too short (so am I, haha) so fuck it! You live once! Life is about enjoying it + not taking it too seriously. Humor is the key. I design t-shirts with midget/disability humor at 6impstore.com. If people don't like who I am they can kiss my ~~handi~~ handicapped ass and stand me up to do it too!

— Bonnie

MR: PWEE · CVWILLOWST
GAME · OVER INDIGO.ST.
GANG×STER·

"Life is like a box of chocolates, you never know what you're gonna get"

Hi. I'm Aimee. In 2003, at age 30, I was diagnosed with Stage IIIc Inflammatory Breast Cancer. I went through 9 cycles of 4 different kinds of chemo, 6 surgeries, 2 stays in the hospital, 35 radiation treatments, and 8 months of weekly monoclonal antibody treatments. I also lost both my breasts. Cancer taught me there's a difference between being cured and being healed. Tattooing for me has been about healing. I never wanted to cover my scars, pretending cancer never happened to me. It's totally about my spiritual journey and each element of my tattoo meta-phorically represents that journey . . . .

Aimee

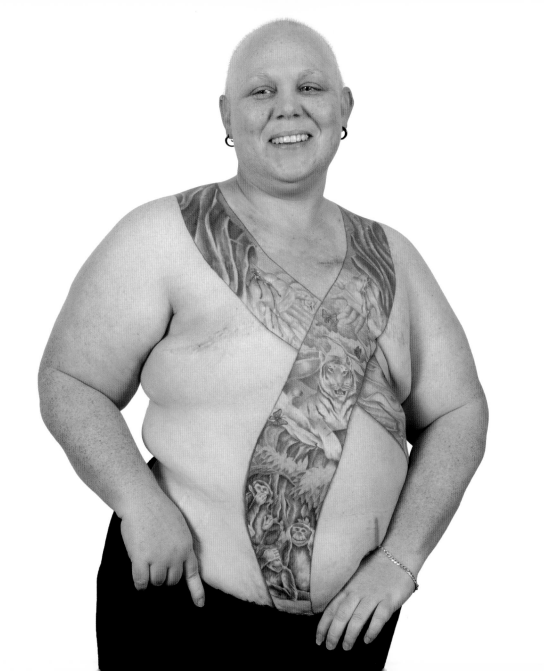

The geisha on my leg was something I've always wanted, but I wanted to find a very talented person to tattoo it. Then I met Horitaka, who was introduced to me by my good friend Pierce. Pierce then wanted to pay for my warrior on my back for my wedding gift. The warrior on my back was all Horitaka's idea. Femire, yet bad ass ... like me!

... Booda (the dog in the Gucci bag) is my baby! ♡

1st Tat2 I ever got.

Not the best Tat2, but Tre most meaning to me. My Grandmother who use to take care of me when my mom and dad left to united states.

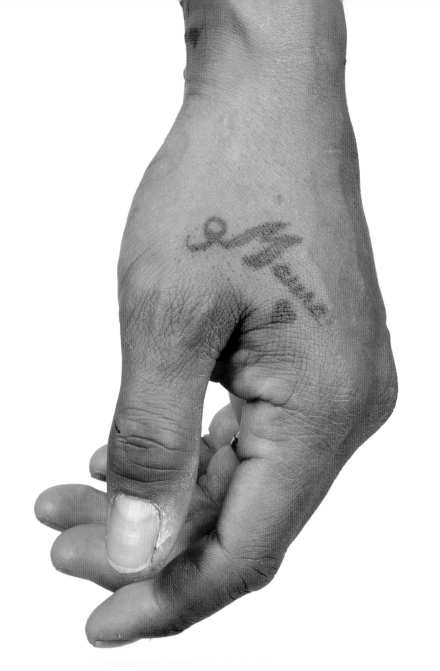

My art is who I am... all the shades of black to grey, with bright color as my smile. Ink is for me, Iatdude for life. My fears are faced head on to get through the fear, and I have been lucky enough to help others along the way. I Save the Boobies... Awareness, Prevention & Survival.

Iats for a Cure
Healing the Heart,
Mind & Soul!

Trance

Interview with Bill Smith

Kip Fulbeck: Mr. Smith, can you tell me about how you came to get your tattoos?

Bill Smith : Well, I signed up for the Marines as soon as I could after we got attacked. I went over there in March, but they wouldn't take me until May.

Why wouldn't they take you?

Because I wouldn't be seventeen until May 28, 1942.

And you said before you didn't weigh enough to get in at first?

Well, I managed . . . was able to push my weight up to 125 by drinking a lot of water and eating bananas—right down to the doctor's office.

How did you choose the Marine Corps over other branches of service?

Well, my father had been a Marine since the, what they called the German-American War—1916. So I was a second generation.

And when did you decide to get the Marine Corps tattoos?

Oh, in New River at boot camp. We had a tattoo parlor right there, a roof over the, what do you call it—an alley. A guy named Ace Harland set up tattoo needles. There was about two bars, and four or five taxis. It was a big delivery town, ya know, with the parlor houses there. Seventh heaven. They raised the pay from $17 to $21 a month, and after that went in, it went up to $35. Then they made it to $50. Fifty dollars a month to spend!

That's a big jump.

It was a land of ten-cent cigarettes and $3 girls. You were loaded.

And how much did the tattoos cost?

Oh, a buck and a half, I guess.

That's great. Did a lot of your fellow corpsmen get tattoos as well?

Whole lot of them, yeah. Some of the guys who had bigger arms got the bulldog, ya know. The big dog, bulldog, with the helmet on, and the spiked collar, USMC.

And how did you pick what to get?

Ah, I just liked the emblem. I don't have a big arm, so I couldn't get the big bull, that big bull-dog wrapped around.

Was it real busy that time in the tattoo parlor?

Well, there was all those guys waiting, so yeah.

And always Marine Corps?

Yeah, it was all Marine Corps. We had naval medics, ya know, they were sailors. They resented the handed-out Marines. I remember one of the doctors when I was in the hospital said, "If you had enough people in the Marines that could read and write, you could have your own medical corps." I thought it was kind of insulting.

So did you ever have any problem with the tattoo up until what happened at the theaters?

No, no. You can see 'em, they're blurry now, ya know. But ex-Marines know what they are right away. "Semper fi, buddy."

So what happened at the movie theater? How'd that come about?

Well, when I was hired we had a nice uniform with a shirt and a bow tie, red vest, black pants. And a few years later, I don't remember just when, they went to the polo shirts, which were a lot cheaper. And, oh, the guys, they all thought the uniform looked great, and now the polo shirt—okay. Now, we had a manager then, from Philadelphia, black lady, very nice. They had that tattoo rule, but she said, "That doesn't affect Bill. He's not going to lose his job." 'Cause I was a bit unusual, more or less. And then, somebody had made some remark about it and she said that

I had that fleece jacket, ya know. She said, "Put that on if any of the big shots are around." So I had that thing there and I'd put it on sometimes if I knew somebody was coming. But then this outfit bought General Cinema out.

Mr. Smith, how old were you when all this was going on?

Well, when I first went to work there I was sixty-five. I had just retired that spring and I decided I didn't like being retired so I took a part-time job. So they had the same written rule about tattoos. And as I had been warned about it—

And the rule was you couldn't show tattoos?

Couldn't show a tattoo on the forearms. If you had tattoos anywhere else that didn't show, they didn't object. But I know I was working away and putting a standee together—you know, those cardboard things with a picture? And I was down on my knees and I heard the manager say to somebody, "There's no key on that box," meaning the doorman's box. But I didn't put any significance on that. And that was the night that the two girls told me that they had to fire me. And I said, "What? I've been working here fifteen years. I never had a write-up. I was never late." And they said it was the tattoo thing. I was in shock.

That's amazing. So what does that have to do with that key thing he was talking about?

Oh, the doorman's box is supposed to have a key, but the lock doesn't work and she was only pointing it out to someone who was not familiar with it. They put two pieces together, this was some guy . . . one of the big wheels from Kansas City.

I see.

Kansas City, now, Wichita, where the hell they are? Anyway, so I went to a lawyer that my wife's friend knows and told him what they did. And he said that was a pretty high-handed thing. And he wrote a letter to the top legal officer of the company and said how the United States was in a state of war and so forth and that this was no way to treat a Marine veteran. And he said we'll give them three or four days to answer.

What happened?

They didn't answer, so right away he got in touch with *Courier News* and told them the story and Sunday afternoon a lady came up with a photographer and took the story and picture. I think it was Tuesday it was in the paper. And the guy that was the manager now said that they don't want you to talk to the media. And I said, "Too late. I talked to the media. It'll be in the papers tomorrow and the television people just left."

That's great.

So the shit hit the fan and then all of a sudden everything was all forgotten and forgiven. Some gentleman from Kansas City—Wichita—wherever the headquarters is, was up here, ostensibly for some other reason. He made a point of coming to me and telling me this shouldn't have happened and apologized and if I would wear something to cover the tattoos so they could keep their, ah, formula. And that wouldn't bother me, no. So I got some sleeves, put 'em on underneath the shirt and that's how that's covered. And I'm there from now on, as far as I want to be. And that's the whole story.

Now, Mr. Smith, how old were you when that actually happened, when they actually fired you?

I guess I was seventy-nine or eighty.

And you had been working there fourteen years?

Ah, I'm in the sixteenth year now. Started a sixteenth year.

That's really an amazing story.

Yeah, I'll be. You know the law is that you can fire anybody. You don't have a union, you got no rights. But there is such a thing as, ah, public outreach—and that works.

That's great.

In fact, I was working yesterday. I work all the holidays and weekends, ya know. Christmas—so people with kids at home could be home. I said I could work. And yesterday, a fellow said, "I'm glad to see you're back. I heard about the case." And there was a woman Thursday said the same thing, that she knew about the whole story. So every day, from the time that happened right around all through the fall I was getting this. A couple people said, "Oh, you should get a lot of money out of this." Actually, you don't have any real rights. Because under the law, in this state, I don't know how bad the rest of 'em are, they can fire anybody for any reason. And unless you can prove racial discrimination or something, you haven't got a case.

And so, they didn't respond to your lawyer at all until you went to the media.

Oh yeah. That's what did it. The legal officer, he should've gotten right on the ball, but he didn't.

Would've saved him a big headache.

Yeah. See, ah, this is a very good attorney and he likes that sort of thing.

It's a great story.

Yeah, well, the public has a lot of power in the service business. And, like a theater, you want people to think you're trying to do a decent thing. Otherwise, they can, there are plenty of other theaters.

And what is your job at the theater, Mr. Smith?

Mainly, I'm a ticket-taker. I greet the people, bounce the kids who misbehave, and like that.

What do you think of tattoos nowadays now that they're so popular?

Well, there's nothing wrong with it as far as I see. And a lot of them get a lot of pointless tattoos and other tattoos mean something. And some of them are just art— artwork. Well, all the different tribes in Melanesia where I was, they tattoo the faces. And on black people it doesn't look bad. But it shows you what family they're in, what village, what tribe, and so forth. And I've known other people get their faces tattooed, too. I would never do that.

Have you seen that really change a lot in the way tattoos are accepted?

Oh, it's changed a lot in that. When I was a young kid, I knew *one* tattooed woman. She was a Paiute Indian woman. She had two, three children that

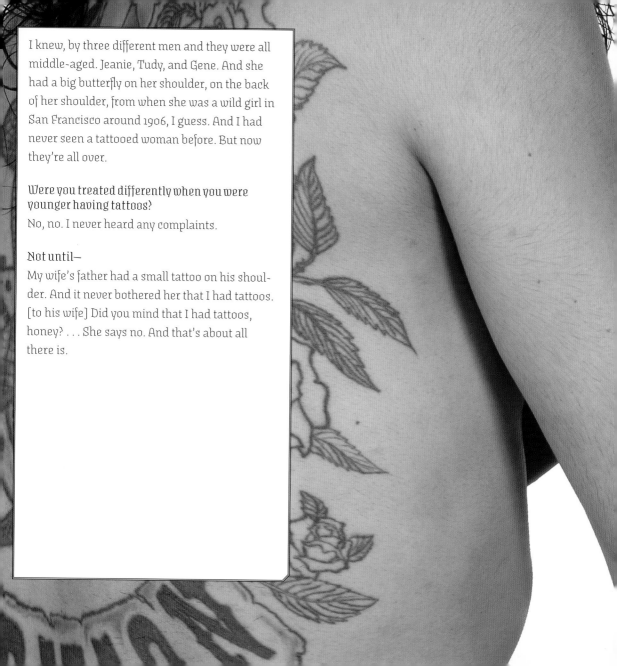

I knew, by three different men and they were all middle-aged. Jeanie, Tudy, and Gene. And she had a big butterfly on her shoulder, on the back of her shoulder, from when she was a wild girl in San Francisco around 1906, I guess. And I had never seen a tattooed woman before. But now they're all over.

Were you treated differently when you were younger having tattoos?
No, no. I never heard any complaints.

Not until—
My wife's father had a small tattoo on his shoulder. And it never bothered her that I had tattoos. [to his wife] Did you mind that I had tattoos, honey? . . . She says no. And that's about all there is.

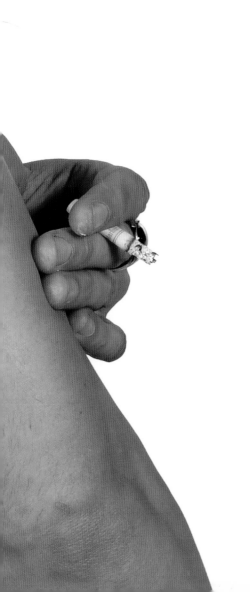

In 1942 I was in the Marines.
We trained on Parris Island, South Carolina.
We were then transfered to New River, No.
Caroline, which now is called Camp Lejune.
At night we went Jacksonville, where many of us
got tattoos. We were proud to be in the Corps.
    Last year I was working for the Cinema
in the local mall. They had a rule "no
visable tattoos" I had been there 15 years,
and never had a repremand, and they fired
me! My son and a lawyer protested: they
got the story in the Courier News, and company
took me back, with back pay, but I have to
have the tattoos covered.

Stephanie and I picked the tattoo parlor because it had a herse parked there. 🚗

♡I named it: "Corndog", for no good reason.... My only reservation was that my "someday husband" would never see me naked→if I get inked.

(Mr Mint, grandma nutt, King Kandy, jolly, plumpy, princess Lolly, queen frostine, Lord licorice, and gloppy the molasses monster)
↳ Remember Candy Land? ☺

The reason 4 me getting Life is Pain was
I was having A lot of problems & ended up in the
hospital 3 times 4 tying to take my own Life.
I was tired of my life & how it was going
& decide to say Life is pain cuz however
you see it you suffer & die Every day for the
rest of your life Also I get tattoos to express
what I feel & to represent were Im from
& wee I come from & where Im headed.
& out of respect to my familia.

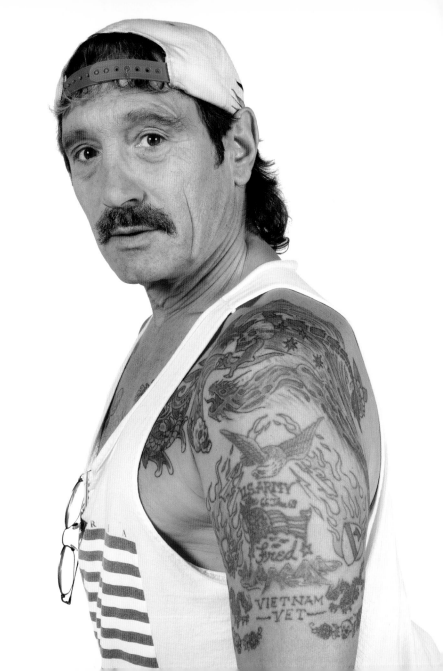

THIS TATTOO WAS STARTED IN 1969
WITH THE FLAG DONE ~~so~~ BY LYLE TUTTLE
IN S.F. ~~AFTER~~ I RETURNED FROM VIET
NAM AFTER SERVING WITH THE ~~FIRST TATOO~~
FIRST AIR CAVALRY. THEN IT GREW--
ALL THE ART ON MY BODY IS A
PIECE OF MY LIFE.

My partner and i had just got into a fight. The morning after we were sitting at a coffee shop looking at each other awkwardly, when she said, "let's go get 'bitch be cool' tattooed on our arms." So we did. It's a motto for life. We're still together.

MY CHEST TATTOO IS A MIX BETWEEN
THE CLASSIC HOMEWARD BOUND MOTIF
AND AN OLD GOSPEL SONG.

MOST OF MY TATTOOS ARE A MIX
OF INFLUENCES — THINGS I LOVE, STUFF
THAT WAS FUNNY AT THE TIME — PEOPLE
OR PLACES I WANT TO REMEMBER . . . .

I JOINED THE ARMY RIGHT OUT OF HIGH SCHOOL WHEN I WAS 18. I MISSED THE SAT SO I THOUGHT I COULDN'T GO TO COLLEGE. WU IS MY LAST NAME AND BANGER WAS DERIVED FROM MY HABIT OF ALWAYS TRYING TO KNOCK THINGS OUT, AND MY COMPETITIVENESS. I JUST CAME BACK FROM A DEPLOYMENT IN GUANTANAMO BAY (GTMO) WHERE I PRETTY MUCH BABYSAT GROWN MEN WHO ARE TRYING TO KILL ME. ITS NOT WHAT IT ALWAYS APPEARS TO SEEM ON THE NEWS ★ WU BANGER

I have three tattoos. The heart
on my leg which has my
husbands name on it. I got it one
romantic night in Paris, and
my two stars, which are a
symbol of my sweet shining
life. I am always reaching for
the stars.

love
and
Just,
XOXO
Teri Patrick

I have worked as a shop bitch for a couple years. I love this industry and want it to contiue to thrive. Books not T.V. shows are the way to keep tattooing alive. I am basically working to become a high school P-E. teacher. I hope that tattooing and tattoos will continve to be somthing that I love throusout my life!

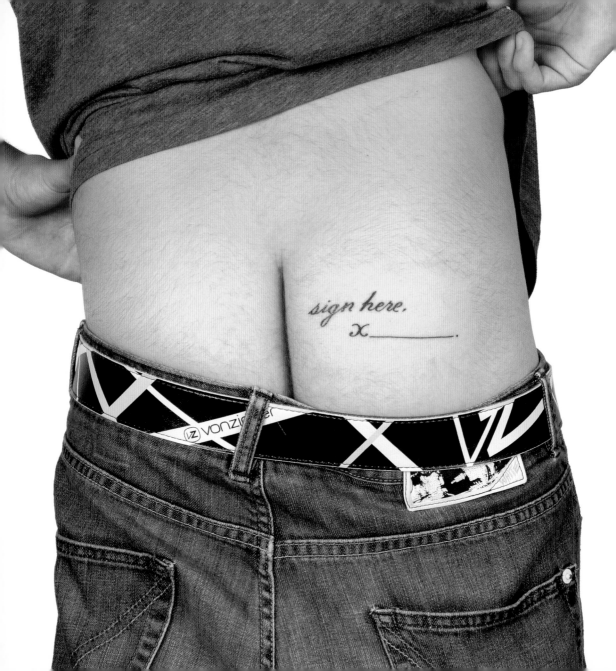

Why they put tattoo parlors
next to Bars I have no idea

After an evening at the bar next door to work with the girls. Lucy who I work with had a great idea that we get anti-straight edge tattoos = ✓✓✓

A good time
not a long time

N✗

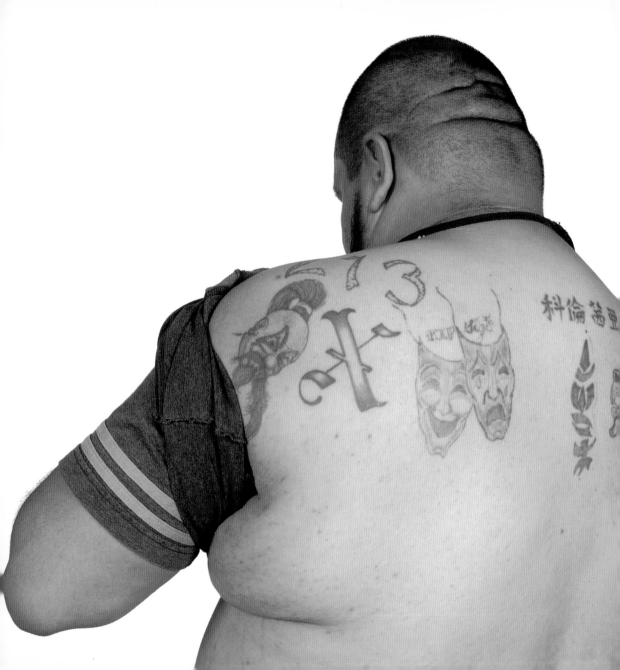

My tattoos are a constant reminder
of a lifestyle I once lived. Today
I have a son who walks me through
those life experiences everytime we
engage eachother about my tattoos.
Every question he asks is a new
life experience for him as much as
for me. Every question he asks is
a historical lesson on the chicano
experience in LA and the world
a lesson on gangs and drugs
a lesson on politics and culture
but most importantly a lesson on
life and living.

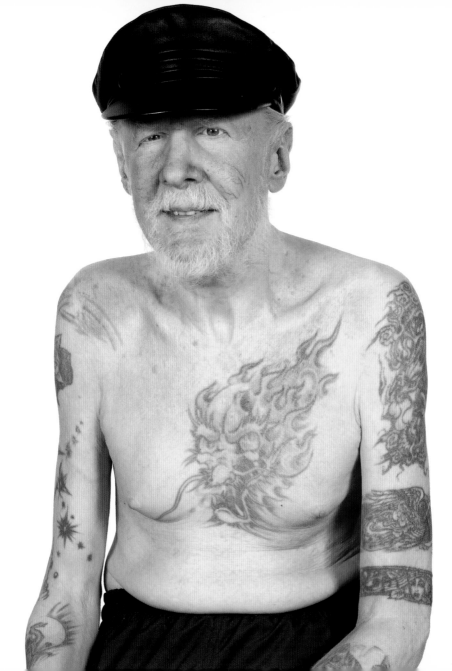

Johnny Winter

<u>Jett</u> - <u>left hip</u>. this is my first, that i got when i was 16 at Lyle Tuttle's Sunset Strip tattoo. Since it was my name, i thought a jett diving into the jungle was appropriate!. i had to hide this with a band aid from Dad for awhile.

<u>V</u> - middle of chest. this is an ornate V, with a diamond seed in the middle. i read that 10,000 to 7,000 yrs ago, some of the first figurines that were ~~discovered~~ discovered to represent divinity had this V mark on the chest. So i put one on me to remind myself that there is divinity in each of us.

<u>spiral</u> - <u>left</u> forearm. - this represents un-manifest consciousness, or consciousness at rest, with the rays coming out representing possibilities

HORIYOSHI III

FOREVER !

I got my Tattoo in Auschwitz
on my 17-ta birthday August 18
1944.
The Germans took me there
only because I _am_ Jewish

I'm A disAbled drummer who's Also 4' TAll. I use crutches to wAlk, my TAHoo is of ANimAl of the muppets A CRAZY DRummer, I've PlAyed for JAmes Brown And George - clinton, yes I'm A midget...

Taking a PIECE of the CARRibean where ever I go!

MY 'PROVIDENCE' TATTOO WITH THE NAUTICAL STAR UNDERNEATH BASICALLY PROMOTES MY LOVE FOR ALL THINGS HAVING TO DO WITH. SEAFARING WHETHER ACTUALLY JUST DOING IT OR READING ABOUT IT (READ ANYTHING ABOUT SHACKLETON OR NANSEN).

'GRACE', 'MAE', AND 'SUSAN FOREVER' ARE ODES TO MY 3 GIRLS. A DAGGER WITH FLAMES IN A TATTOO ARE ALWAYS COOL TO ME... OLD SCHOOL.

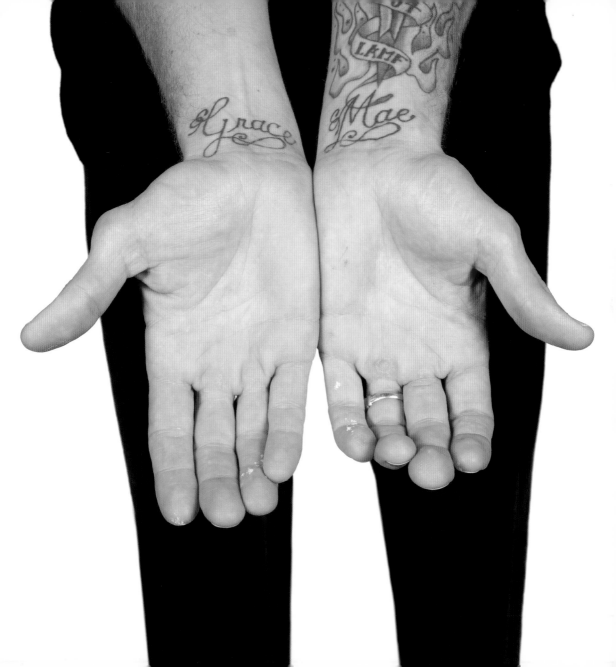

I AM "TRUE TO THE GAME".

Featured Participants

Nancy Ahn
Al Albarran
Cix Allender
Sebastian Allender
Kris Andrews
Anonymous
Jimmy Arnett
Carlinda Atkinson
Mike Atkinson
Richie Belton
Chris Bradford
Eva Brown
Jim Burnett
Tiernach Cassidy
James Castillo
Silvestre Chavez
Samantha Chin-Wolner
Austin Cho
Margaret Cho
Andrew Cornish
Jesse Lee Denning
Travis Diebolt
David Donikian
Donnell Duffie
Winnie Duffie
Jason Dung
Caitlin Dunham
John Evans
Brittany Farmer
Daniel Ferreira
Christopher Flippin
Bugsy Flores
Roman Flores

Jack Frost
Kip Fulbeck
France Garcia
Chris Garver
Terry Gingles
Rhian Gittins
Chet Glaze
Rob Gray
Grime
Saroj Groebler
Armando Gudiño
Tona Hamashige
Beth Harrell
Kelley Henning
Horitaka
Horitomo
Horiyuki
Kara Houston
Jon Huerta
Scott Ian
Adrian Jackson
Marcus Jackson
Joan Jett
Jason Lemieux
Kurt Levee
May-Har Li
Chuck Liddell
Milton Love
Nikole Lowe
Bonnie Malcolm
Christi McGuire
Duff McKagan
Georgia Michel
Chelsea Moore
Gavin Moscon

Sabrina Moscon
Sabrina Motley
Christian Mount
Cindy Mune
Kym Nathan
Julio Nava
Dan Nazzareta
Gina Ngo
Betty Nice
David Oropeza
Annie Orth
Alex Padilla
Keith Palumbo
Tera Patrick
Oliver Peck
Michelle Pedersen
Greg Perez
Fred Pisturino
Holli Porreca
Mark Pulver
Shi Reeves
Pascal Riff-Raff
Ryann Robinson
Michelle Rooy
Mike Rubin
Jamie Ruth
Koji Sakai
David Salles
Joe Samatua
Eric Sardinas
Liz Schiller
Harrison Sebelia
Jeffery Sebelia
Evan Seinfeld
Aimee Shaw

Al Shaw
Edith Singer
Slash
Bill Smith
Nikki Sonesen
Malia Spanyol
Splinter
Paul Stanley
Natalie Studzinski
Anu Tagara
Josh Thomas
Tony Tieu
Jules Tupas
James Tyrell
David Velasquez
Michael Velasquez
Dolores Vallejo
James Vallejo
Vivian Vargas
Monica Vega
Kat Von D
Shannon Walker
Scott Weiland
Sean Wheeler
Beth Wilson
Kate Wilson
Johnny Winter
Pwee Witrago
Gabe Wu
Dan Wysuph
John Zayac
Ronald Zulueta